Dr Sarah Woodhouse is a research psychologist and trauma expert who grew up and trained in the UK, and now lives in Australia with her husband and three children. Her research explores how different ways of thinking, feeling and being can affect trauma symptoms. In her work, Sarah uses her knowledge and her personal experience to help people break free from their past and reclaim their lives.

you're not broken

Break free from **trauma** & reclaim your **life**

Dr Sarah Woodhouse

PENGUIN LIFE

UK | USA | Canada | Ireland | Australia
India | New Zealand | South Africa | China

Penguin Life is part of the Penguin Random House group of companies whose addresses can be found at global.penguinrandomhouse.com

Penguin
Random House
Australia

First published by Penguin Life in 2021

Cover design by James Rendall © Penguin Random House Australia Pty Ltd
Cover image courtesy of Getty Images
Author photograph by Good Thanks Media
Internal design by Midland Typesetters, Australia
Typeset in 9/11 pt Berkeley LT by Midland Typesetters, Australia
Index compiled by Puddingburn

Printed and bound in Australia by Griffin Press, an accredited
ISO AS/NZS 14001 Environmental Management Systems printer

A catalogue record for this
book is available from the
National Library of Australia

ISBN 978 1 76104 016 0

penguin.com.au

This book is dedicated to my children, Roo, Fern and Wren. You have taught me what love, faith, strength, courage and freedom truly mean. Thank you x

Contents

Introduction

I've seen a lot of different therapists over the years. Some were great, some good, and some worryingly bad. When I was twenty-three, one of the great ones said to me:

'Every symptom and issue you bring to me, Sarah, makes me believe that you carry trauma. I think something happened in your past that made you deeply overwhelmed and afraid, and you're still reacting to it.'

I stared at her in stunned silence. I'd had a stable upbringing. I'd been to a good school. I was struggling, yes, but I hadn't been through anything *traumatic*.

Once I regained my composure I decided I'd better set her straight. 'You've got it totally wrong,' I told her firmly. 'I don't have trauma.'

'Okay,' she said. And I pretty much left there and then.

My defensive *how-dare-you* response to the therapist's suggestion that I carried trauma was about my own denial. But it also reflects a wider cultural fear of what trauma means. Within mainstream culture, three false-truths about trauma persist. First, that trauma is a *disorder*. Second, that trauma only happens to an unlucky few who experience very extreme events and symptoms. Third, that trauma permanently damages us, leaving us fundamentally broken.

The result of these misperceptions is, of course, that many of us are afraid of the word. We push it away, when really what we need to do is move towards it so we can better understand it.

Trauma is a protective human *reaction,* not a disorder. Post-traumatic Stress *Disorder* (PTSD) is the name clinical psychologists and psychiatrists have given to high levels of trauma that are prolonged, but it's just a name.

The fact remains that trauma is a reaction, and this is true whether the reaction is more or less severe. (For some reason they lost sight of this as they labelled it in the 1970s.) This reaction can be a response to extreme events, but it can also be a response to common everyday experiences. Maybe the incident was relatively *small*: one we didn't label as traumatic at the time, but as time goes on we can see the lasting effect isn't *small* at all. To a greater or lesser extent, we've all experienced this traumatic reaction. It's part of being human – it unifies us. And far from leaving us fundamentally broken, understanding our own traumatic reactions can lead to our greatest transformation. As we move towards the thing we've been pushing away, we break free and reclaim our life.

When we *don't* recognise how traumatic experiences have affected us, we remain bound to the past and disconnected from our true selves. We're trapped in painful old reactions, patterns and self-limiting traumatic beliefs.

Perhaps something happened that didn't feel at all *okay*, but you laughed it off? Perhaps you can't remember exactly what happened, but you just know there's something there, something you've been afraid to look back at? You're happy to admit things could be better; that you're struggling a little, but – *trauma*? That just sounds too much, too serious, too something-that-happens-to-veterans.

I was afraid for a long time too. My fear held me back from living a full, free, authentic life. Incredible growth is possible once we're brave enough to consider the idea that maybe (just maybe) the difficulties we're experiencing today are connected to our own past traumas. Once we do, and as our understanding grows, we change. We stop feeling afraid of the past. We see the patterns we're stuck in. We see, as clear as day, how the past has affected our self-belief, thoughts, feelings, choices, even our body. We shift from confusion to clarity, and with that clarity comes freedom and growth, coupled with empowerment and thriving.

So, what's a trauma?

Determining what constitutes a *traumatic experience* is more difficult than you might imagine, because an experience is only a trauma if we have a *traumatic reaction*. If we have an upsetting experience, but never have a traumatic reaction to it, it's not one of our traumas. It's the reaction that matters; that defines whether an experience is a trauma.

Any distressing experience – particularly those that occurred in childhood – that you perceived as threatening and extremely overwhelming can provoke a traumatic reaction. This includes experiences that are very severe and disturbing, but also includes often overlooked, everyday experiences and ones that threaten our need for social connection (like feeling unseen, unheard or unloved). The experience sets off a chain of reactions in our body and mind. The reactions set off more reactions, and over time we become stuck in reactive patterns and cycles. Stuck in feelings, sensations, thoughts, beliefs and behaviours. Although painful – and demoralising at times – the repetition and stagnation show us what we need to do to heal.

This book will help you understand all forms of traumatic reactions – from the extreme to those that are more insidious and hard to spot. You'll understand trauma on your own terms, as it relates to your life. Because that's the truth – only you can ever really determine if an experience, a moment, a school, a relationship, a job, a holiday, a conversation, was traumatic. Only you can, because only you can see the truth of your reaction. Once you learn to recognise your traumatic reactions (which I'm going to teach you), you'll better understand your past. You'll also better understand yourself today, and clearly see the roadblocks that are preventing you from moving forward.

No matter where you're currently *stuck*, this book will help you understand your past traumas, recognise your own personal reactions to them, and get *unstuck* – though I would urge anyone who has very high, debilitating, levels of trauma symptoms to seek professional face-to-face support. Primarily, this book is for people who are getting on with their lives, largely unaware of how the trauma they carry affects the way they live their life. It's to help people shift from confusion to clarity about themselves and their problems. To help people shift from fear to hope, repetition to spontaneity, reaction to action, powerlessness to empowerment, from *stuck* to freedom and growth.

Trauma affects everything

I think the single most important thing I learnt during the ten years I researched trauma as an academic is that trauma affects everything. This may sound like an overstatement, but it's not. You only need to take a brief look at the lengthy list of trauma symptoms in the Appendix (p. 223) and you'll see what I mean. The symptoms, behaviours, moods, coping mechanisms, thoughts and feelings that we now know link directly to trauma are extremely broad (and growing). As well as the list of symptoms that are directly associated with trauma, there is growing research linking other aspects of wellbeing and mental health to previous trauma.[1]

Did you see the Russell Brand quote that went around social media?

Cannabis isn't a gateway drug. Alcohol isn't a gateway drug. Nicotine isn't a gateway drug. Caffeine isn't a gateway drug.

Trauma is the gateway. Childhood abuse is the gateway. Molestation is the gateway. Neglect is the gateway.

What Russell Brand so eloquently highlights is that childhood trauma commonly leads to a heap of negative outcomes for the kids involved. Research has shown that adverse (shitty, abhorrent, unfair) childhood experiences[2] increase a child's likelihood of developing certain physical problems in adulthood, including strokes, liver disease, chronic lung disease, diabetes, cancer, headaches, gastrointestinal problems and obesity.[3] I think these physical outcomes are mind-blowing. And as you would expect, adverse childhood experiences and trauma can also lead to cognitive, emotional and behavioural issues. Learning and behavioural problems, depression, eating disorders, anxiety, smoking, PTSD, various psychiatric disorders, risky sexual behaviour and addiction are all associated, to a greater or lesser degree, with traumatic childhood experiences.[4]

To summarise: trauma in childhood affects our mind and body. Some of you know this is true because you're living with one or more of the outcomes I've just covered. But a lot of us dismiss uncomfortable facts like these. For many, our denial is so strong that we're unable to engage with reality: 'I wasn't *properly* neglected as a kid. No liver disease here.' Our denial, resistance and avoidance makes this whole topic about other people. But it's not. It's *about* a lot of people. That's the whole point.

There's no escaping the reality that if we've experienced trauma – as so many have – but have had no treatment and done no work, trauma is still likely to be affecting our lives. The research I've mentioned above is just the tip of the iceberg, because this is broader than labels and conditions and diagnoses. It's about our day-to-day life – our ability to experience joy, our willingness to trust ourselves, our confidence and self-esteem. It's about our contentment, or lack of it. It's about our sense of purpose, and why we get up in the morning. It's about being able to be in the moment. It's about laughter and love.

What do you think your past traumas affect? Your beliefs? Your opinions? Your choice of partner? Your choice of friends? Your hobbies (or lack of them)? Your choice of career? Your willingness to socially interact? Your ability to socially interact? Your ability to trust? To love? To commit? To share? To open up? Your willingness to learn? To be around men? To be around women? To parent? To hold down a job? To love yourself? To see your potential? To what? How does your past trauma affect your life? This sits at the heart of what this book is really about: real life, and ways to make it better.

As we all do

I firmly believe that we're drawn to certain things in life – careers, people, countries, books, movies, anything – that somehow serve us spiritually and psychologically. I'm one of those irritating people who thinks everything has a meaning and that very little in our lives happens by accident. I'm a researcher, and researchers find patterns. We'd be terrible at our jobs if our conclusions were that everything is a coincidence and life is a chaotic mess. I was drawn to research because I believe that through logically observing life we can learn and grow. We can find the meaning humans have accidentally or deliberately embedded into their actions, words and lives. My choice of career has a personal meaning to me and serves me on various levels. It serves the part of my soul that needs to be of service, to help others heal and grow. And on a less enlightened note, it serves the part of me that's a perfectionist and needs external validation. Meaning and motive isn't always pure, but it's there.

Remember that therapist I saw when I was twenty-three? The one who dared to suggest I carry trauma? After I walked out of that session, I did what I do best: I intellectualised the problem. I left my career in lobbying to study psychology, specialising in . . . guess what?! Trauma! This isn't a joke, I actually did do this. Why feel your feelings or own your truth when you can run statistical analyses?! I determinedly flew through my Master of Science, receiving first-class honours for my research into how thinking affects trauma symptoms. After a couple of years working in rehab centres and on different research projects (all studying trauma, obviously), I applied to do a PhD. In total I spent ten years researching trauma in academia, single-mindedly fixated on figuring *the problem* out.

I'm not exaggerating, or saying this to entertain you. This incredible display of denial and subconscious motivation is the truth of my life. Someone suggested that I carried trauma, and instead of facing it, I decided I was going to think my way out of the problem. It didn't work, and somewhere between statistical analyses 456 and 527, I admitted that maybe I could do with a bit of help. I wasn't falling apart in the way I had when I was younger, but I knew things weren't right. I often found friendships and romantic relationships confusing and painful. I spaced out and felt like I was floating if I felt socially uncomfortable. I was anxious more often than I wasn't. I became stressed and overwhelmed by the smallest interruption to my daily plan. I was, once more, using under-eating as a way to cope. The major difference at this time in my life, compared to when I was twenty-three, was that I was in a relationship that I really wanted to go the distance. And honestly, I knew in my bones that unless I began making meaningful changes, the life I wanted wouldn't happen.

I went back to the same therapist I saw at twenty-three, and at the same time I worked on a program around my food and eating disorder. I practised yoga and meditation daily and developed a deep spirituality and faith. I was changing, opening up and reconnecting with my body. I was gently, somewhat hesitantly, realising that perhaps statistical analyses didn't have all the answers.

In the years since, I've worked with other great therapists and practitioners. Working with one therapist in particular (who quite possibly is the most patient woman on the planet) changed me. This work, which took time and courage, is why I'm writing this book instead of applying for another research grant. I've got more research in me, that's for sure, but now the numbers will always be translated back into meaningful, accessible words on the page. Back into feelings, back into a form that can help us all rise up and out of our trauma.

It's the human being part of me, as an individual who has experienced traumas and has had a varied (and somewhat epic) healing journey, that leads me to really *know* what I'm talking about. I'm not just a researcher who has drawn conclusions from literature reviews and scientific hypothesising. I am a human who has had her own journey. As we all do.

Resistance

The bigger the resistance, the greater the transformation. Have you heard that before? It's a beautiful phrase. It contains such truth and wisdom. It's not my phrase, by the way, but it is one of my favourite recovery phrases. What does it mean? It means that our greatest personal transformations will come about by moving *towards* those aspects of life that we have the most resistance to. Our ego tells us not to open the box. Don't try and find new solutions . . . don't put yourself out there . . . don't make yourself vulnerable . . . don't go there. Our ego, fuelled by our trauma, wants us to stay where we are because it's what it believes is safe. It's wrong.

My resistance prevented me from working with the therapist when I was twenty-three. The resistance in this example isn't hard to spot, right?! I walked out. But not all resistance is as obvious. Take my resistance to intimacy and vulnerability. It showed up in all kinds of stealthy ways. It was my need to be entertaining, no matter my mood. It showed up when I walked away from a relationship with an open-hearted, loving man because it felt *too much*, too suffocating. It's why I wouldn't call friends if I was struggling – I'd wait until I was able to crack a joke, and then I'd call. It was when I couldn't sit in a moment holding a gaze, instead looking away because it felt too uncomfortable. Of course, my resistance to intimacy and vulnerability was also one of the reasons I walked out on that therapist. It felt too intimate, too insightful and too 'I see you, Sarah'.

But at one point or another I begrudgingly moved towards the things I was resisting, and the truth of what they represented for me. When I say 'begrudgingly' I mean that sometimes it was years of resistance, avoidance and denial. I'm as stubborn as anyone you've ever met. Worse, I pretend not to be because I know it's really unenlightened. I'm a stubborn control freak, masquerading as someone who goes with the flow! So prior to accepting and looking at the many, *many* things I resisted, I was saying or thinking something along the lines of, '100 per cent that's not a problem for me, so get lost'. Nice. I would undermine things I resisted – belittle them, push them away, overcompen-sate and pretend. I would get defensive and self-righteous. I would make excuses, hesitate, make a joke. These were all manifestations of my resistance, fuelled by my fear of change. I would go so far, then stop, put my fingers in my ears and pretend I had everything figured out.

The behaviours I've described are all common psychological reactions to change and growth. People do this stuff all the time, day in day out. It's part of being human, and something we all need to consider if we want to grow. Change necessarily entails resistance – the two are painfully and intimately entwined. So don't expect to skip through trauma healing. Sometimes we limp. Sometimes we sit down and take a rest because the resistance and the energy required to overcome it is just too much. But don't let your resistance to healthy change derail you. See it, feel it, have a good old swear and a cry if you need, then send it on its way.

My traumas were the springboard for my greatest transformation, and yours can be too. Call it trauma, give it the death stare, and you will grow stronger than you could ever have imagined possible. You will embody resilience. You will find freedom and growth. You will thrive.

The principles of trauma healing

Many people get in touch with me asking how they can heal their trauma. It's the question I'm asked the most and it's the driving force behind this book. The relief people feel as they step into their truth, calling it trauma for the first time, is often replaced with overwhelm as they sense that healing from trauma is a rather imprecise art. This is the truth and I can't pretend otherwise. Trauma is about us all, yes, but our healing journeys are unique to us. That's not to say we do it alone. Far from it – I counted up all the people who have helped me heal over the years, from those in support groups to therapists, body workers, coaches and more, and in total there were more than 160 people. I'm still counting, because I lean on people and I learn from people, to this day. This is how I heal, how I grow and expand.

So I'm not saying that we do it alone, but I am saying that at the outset we should acknowledge there's no *right* way to heal. Although similarities exist in the journeys of those I've spoken with over the years, there are also huge variations. Some find deep healing through dance, others through cognitive behavioural therapy (CBT). Some heal through yoga, others with Eye Movement Desensitization and Reprocessing (EMDR). Some with long-term psychotherapy, others with short-term somatic (body) work. Some use medication, others do not. Some find deep healing through their spiritual awakening, others through exercise and routine. Some use meditation, others use movement. Some use healing circles, others go on retreats. Some (in fact, most) use a unique mix of support and therapies that suit them. There are endless ways to heal. It's the principles that matter, not the detail.

Although there's no *right* way to heal, it always involves:

- **body** work to help us connect to our body and heal our physical and emotional reactions
- healing our **mind** by deepening our understanding, transforming our traumatic thinking and subconscious beliefs, and gently processing our past experiences
- shifting out of self-limiting **behaviours**, traumatic coping and life patterns and

- **reconnection** to our unbreakable core, our higher self and our instinct.

These are the principles I was referring to: body, mind, behaviours and reconnection. Whatever our journey, wherever it takes us, all four need to be given space and attention when we're ready.

The book is split into three parts. Part one teaches you about trauma and traumatic reactions. Part two helps you figure out how trauma affects different areas of your life – relationships, health and work. Part three is all about looking forward – resilience, breaking free and reclaiming your life. If you're anything like me, you're going to want to jump straight to part three so you can get to the answers, 'fix' yourself, and move on to the next self-help book. But the real growth comes from learning to spot a traumatic reaction. So stand down. Turn to the next page. Start at the start.

Part 1

Understanding trauma

Chapter One

What is a trauma?

A trauma can only be defined by our reactions. An event is only horrifying because we're horrified, or scary because we're scared. Without a reaction, an event is just a moment in time. We all react differently to different events – so my traumas will not necessarily be your traumas, and vice versa. Trauma *is* relational (meaning we react to something) but it's also a primarily internal experience. As Dr Gabor Maté, the world-renowned trauma expert, explains: the trauma happens *in* us, not *to* us.[1]

My explanation of trauma leaves room for *your* unique response to *your* trauma. Yes, there will be shared feelings, processes, understanding and healing with others on this journey, but your trauma will always be personal to you. I'm stating this truth now, to empower you to begin observing your reactions. Become interested and curious in your past reactions and your reactions today.

In the box below, I've given you four definitions of trauma, each of which offers a different *way in* to understanding trauma. Each definition can stand alone, but together they provide a full explanation of trauma.

Following these definitions, I've gone into more detail about each of them. I've also outlined some context about where these definitions have come from, because I want you to know that what I'm saying isn't radically new. What is radically new is my way of pulling it together.

Trauma – four definitions

1. A trauma is a *perceived threat* that overwhelms us and our ability to respond.
2. Trauma is our *unprocessed memory* of the experience.
3. Trauma is our ongoing *cycle* of traumatic reactions, and our attempts to cope with these reactions and manage our feelings.
4. Trauma is our *disconnection* from our sense of self, others and the world that follows the traumatic experience.

---

1. A trauma is a *perceived threat* that overwhelms us and our ability to respond

This first definition reflects the work of somatic psychologists, psychotherapists and researchers who focus on the body, and the body–mind connection. The somatic (body-led) branch of trauma healing tells us that the human survival response is at the centre of a traumatic reaction. Dr Peter Levine has explained that trauma develops because we perceive a threat to be too big for us to properly respond to, so as well as feeling an intense sense of threat we also feel extremely overwhelmed.[2] The sense of an overwhelming threat, plus the flood of arousal hormones from the fight or flight response, often leads to feelings of powerlessness, helplessness or shut down (freeze). Once the fight, flight, freeze response is switched on, it remains active long after the threat. I've gone into greater detail about this process in chapter three.

2. Trauma is our *unprocessed memory* of the experience

The second definition highlights the central role of memory dysfunction in trauma. This is a meaty subject area and can get really academic, so we'll try not to get bogged down in details. Led by Dr Francine Shapiro, this area of treatment has taught us that memories of a traumatic experience are not properly formed and processed.[3] The intense fight, flight, freeze response interferes with our ability to think, so instead of being processed (understood and assimilated) down into our long-term memory banks, the memories are stored in a way that still connects them to the initial emotion, physical sensations and beliefs. This leads to them popping up at seemingly random times. The unprocessed memories are active, intense and easily triggered.

3. Trauma is our ongoing *cycle* of traumatic reactions, and our attempts to cope with these reactions and manage our feelings

Trauma traps us in cycles. In my own research I include *feedback loops* in my trauma models (statistical diagrams of how trauma develops). This means there isn't a nice, neat, causal line from one thing to the next that ends with a tidy outcome. Instead, the outcomes feed back to the original cause. Trauma is messy and circular, so these feedback loops help explain how traumatic reactions develop. For example, a traumatic experience leads to physical trauma symptoms and overwhelming emotions, leading to traumatic thinking, which in turn leads to self-defeating coping mechanisms. This outcome, dysfunctional coping, first enables us to avoid and disconnect from our difficult feelings. Over time, though, our dysfunctional coping can end up making our physical symptoms or overwhelming emotions worse. This then leads to more traumatic thinking, and on and on.[4] The idea of a cyclical Trauma Loop (and breaking it) is central to this book and to your growth. In chapter three, I explain in greater detail what happens at each stage of the Trauma Loop.

4. Trauma is our *disconnection* from our sense of self, others and the world that follows the traumatic experience

Every aspect of the traumatic reaction, from the initial over-whelm to our traumatic coping, *disconnects* us somehow from ourselves, others and the world. The fourth definition reflects Professor Ronnie Janoff-Bulman's shattered assumptions theory of trauma,[5] and the more recent writings of Dr Gabor Maté.[6] During a traumatic experience, our survival response leads to varying levels of disconnection from our body, our mind, our feelings, our experience and our sense of self. Later traumatic reactions serve to increase this sense of disconnection from self, and move us further away from our feelings, as a way of coping. The reactions and changes in our beliefs (*I'm bad, the world isn't safe, people can't be trusted*) also serve to disconnect us from others, our support networks and the world as we know it. Moving past trauma always involves reconnection. We'll expand on this in chapter three.

Unprocessed memory?! Whaaaaat?

The definitions above are a bit abstract. They reflect complicated processes that can be hard to relate to. But I have to include them. Although I'm determined to make this topic as accessible as possible, I also know that knowledge is power when it comes to trauma.

Trauma really is an unprocessed memory. Think for a moment about how old *stuff* shows up in your own life. Do *old* difficult feelings, thoughts, beliefs, sensations or images repeatedly intrude on your life? If so, it's likely they link to a memory that hasn't been properly processed.

To help illustrate the whole odd, abstract idea of unprocessed memory, I want to talk about Jenn. Obviously, she's not actually called Jenn, but everything else about this story is real. I met Jenn at a mother and baby group just after I'd given birth to my son. We were both new mums and bonded over our overwhelming, beautiful, intense transition to motherhood. When Jenn's daughter was about three years old, Jenn started to really struggle. Whenever she was not physically with her daughter, even for very short periods of time, Jenn's chest became tight and she struggled to breathe. Negative thoughts would race through her head: *My daughter is in danger, she is unsafe, I can't protect her*. Her GP diagnosed her with generalised anxiety and prescribed medication – which she dutifully took.

Jenn and I met up one afternoon at a children's soft-play centre. After we'd settled down and the kids were happily bouncing around, she broke down and told me about the weekend she'd just spent with her mother, Ruth, who had been highly critical of how Jenn was parenting her daughter. Ruth had told Jenn she was too soft and that her 'mental state' was having dire consequences on her daughter's wellbeing.

Ruth had also told Jenn a story about Jenn's own childhood. She explained that because Jenn's father hadn't been around, she'd had to raise Jenn in a practical, no-nonsense way. She'd sleep trained her efficiently and focused on discipline and structure. When Jenn was about three years old, Ruth got a promotion at work that meant she was working long hours, five days a week. Because of the change in her mother's working hours, Jenn left the local preschool she was happy at and was sent to a much bigger childcare centre. Ruth admitted that Jenn didn't like the centre at all.

She would scream hysterically at drop-off and was often distressed when Ruth came back at the end of the day. The centre was honest and told Ruth that Jenn clung fearfully to the staff, and was jumpy and tearful throughout most of the day. This behaviour continued for nearly nine months, and even after this time would often reappear. Despite this, and in large part because Ruth felt she had no other choice, Jenn continued at the centre until she was four-and-a-half years old and started school.

As Jenn and I sat in this loud, frenetic soft-play centre watching our crazy toddlers, I gently suggested to Jenn that her current anxiety might stem from her own experience at three years old. It's hard to explain the intricacies of unprocessed traumatic memory when surrounded by noisy kids, so I just suggested she read up on it. I gave her the name of some books and I also said what I believe to be true – *It's okay. Honestly, it means you know what you're dealing with and can move past it.* Jenn did read up on it. She came to understand that she had unprocessed traumatic memories from childhood. Her memories of herself as a three-year-old were stored in her mind in a way that connected them to the feelings, sensations and beliefs she experienced at the pre-school. Her memory process – the encoding and storage of life experiences – had gone awry because of her intense, overwhelming sense of threat at being left somewhere she didn't feel safe. Fast-forward thirty years and Jenn's unprocessed memories, along with the painful, negative feelings, sensations and beliefs, were regularly triggered when she said goodbye to her own three-year-old daughter. Jenn learnt this through a lot of hard work. She worked with a great psychotherapist who incorporated gentle body-work into their sessions, and she had EMDR therapy (a specific therapy to help deal with unprocessed traumatic memories). She stopped her meds. She put down some healthy boundaries with her mother, and moved on.

I need to add here that toddler-Jenn's prolonged three-year-old reaction to the childcare centre her mother moved her to, all those years ago, was extreme and unusual. Most children happily attend day care and come out with paintings for the wall, not trauma. So if you're a parent reading this, don't unnecessarily worry about the effect of childcare on your kids. As a mum of three, I one hundred per cent relate to that anxious, stomach-clenching knot, but please hear what I said: Jenn's childhood reaction was extreme and unusual. If you're concerned about your child, I recommend reading Peter Levine and Maggie Kline's *Trauma-Proofing Your Kids*.[7] And of course, if you believe your child is experiencing a traumatic reaction, please get professional support. Today, as I write, Jenn is an awesome, inspiring, healthy woman. She did her work. You can too. And so can your kids, if they need to.

Before you move on, take a look below. I asked my followers on Twitter to define trauma. The wisdom and honesty in their responses are staggering, so I've included some here. Whether you're mentioned here or not, thank you to all who contributed.

Twitter's definitions of trauma

Attempting to understand or define trauma to me is equivalent to describing love to someone that has never experienced it. It is not a singular moment, more of a life altering experience that bleeds into every part of who you are and no one experience is the same. @Taylor_made4_ME

A pattern of mental and physical responses focused on increasing probability of survival. @denuya

Our bodies response to our boundaries being broken. @spacedoutsmiles

A distressing experience or set of experiences that threatens a person's real or felt safety to such a degree that it overwhelms an individual's capacity to cope in healthy ways. @MsJenAlexander

Trauma is a discordant vibrational state in matter or energy system caused by interruption beyond that system's ability to assimilate, normalize or regain balance. @photodrumguy

Trauma: a parasite inside my brain that sees fit to fuck up my day/week/month as and when it feels like it. @RTimoclea

Trauma is being subjected to pain and suffering that is beyond your control . . . and deeply affects you emotionally and interferes with your ability to function in a healthy way. @grow_your_wings

Exposure to a highly distressing/disturbing event that cannot be incorporated into a person's sense of self and/or world view. @dorizener

Perceived threat, overwhelm and powerlessness

Here's another way of looking at trauma:

Traumatic experience = Perceived threat + Overwhelm + Powerlessness

That odd but very satisfying little equation is the first part of my explanation of trauma, rejigged and remastered. This equation sits at the heart of how we're going to understand traumatic experiences in this book.

Think for a moment about the first part of the equation: *perceived* threat. Can you sense the subjectivity? What I perceive as threatening isn't necessarily the same thing you might perceive as threatening. Perhaps I grew up in a house with a father terrified of heights, who taught me (both subconsciously and consciously) that heights (small or large) are a major threat to life. So, if I, as an adult, see that my child has climbed to the top of a tree, I will perceive the threat to be huge compared to someone who wasn't conditioned this way. Or perhaps, like many children, I have been taught to fear strangers knocking at the door, so when I'm five years old and a stranger knocks at the door, I will likely perceive the threat to be very large compared to a child who has not experienced this. Our parents' fears very often stem from their own traumatic experiences. They hand them down to us, without realising that they're paving the way for their children's traumatic reactions.

The subjectivity of threat perception is not just about what we're taught as children. It's also about what we learn through our own unique life experiences – what I've learnt may harm me compared to what you've learnt may harm you. Yes, all humans perceive some common threats (a tsunami, someone coming at us with a knife, etc.), many of which are on the list of extreme events included later in this chapter (pp. 32 and 33). But many other experiences are subjectively threatening rather than ubiquitously perceived as threatening to everyone.

Onto the next part of the equation: overwhelm. We might intuitively know what it means, but I think we should pin it down as best we can. Essentially 'overwhelm' means overload. We're flooded with something. We're swamped and submerged in . . . what? A perception, a feeling, or a sense that something is too big for us to handle. We're overwhelmed by our perception of our to-do list, for example. The list *feels* too much for us to handle. Subconsciously or consciously, we've assessed that we don't have the skills, time, energy or aptitude to handle the to-do list, so we feel overwhelmed.

In the context of trauma, this means we're overwhelmed by our perception of a threat that appears (or is) too big for us to handle. The experience feels too extreme for us to understand or respond to, and most likely it is. The sense of overwhelm isn't static – it grows and grows as our fight, flight, freeze response kicks in (more on this in chapter three). We're flooded with hormones. We're overloaded by our own response. We're overwhelmed.

Now onto powerlessness. This aspect of the traumatic reaction is intricately connected to the other two. Perceiving a threat as too big for us to handle and feeling extremely overwhelmed often leads to a sense of powerlessness and helplessness. During or after a traumatic experience we feel vulnerable, unsure, shocked and fragile. We feel small and wounded, deflated. Many also feel put in their place, shamed, embarrassed or 'less-than'.

The difficulty is that our feelings of powerlessness and helplessness often quickly transform into denial or anger, so for some it can feel like a hard concept to find peace with. Angry, deeply hurt people shout their pain and reach for power. Because they were made to feel powerless, they do everything they can today to ensure they don't feel it again. But they aren't empowered; they're still trapped in their old reaction.

Reclaiming our power is a critical part of the healing journey. We must consider how our ongoing or triggered powerlessness is affecting our lives today. Perhaps we give up, perhaps we don't try, perhaps we settle for less than we deserve. Perhaps we become apathetic, perhaps we walk away or shut down. Perhaps we accept abuse or neglect. Or perhaps we overpower and try to control others, because we're still trapped in our old reactions. Either way, stepping into our real authentic self, and therefore connecting to our real power, is a critical part of freedom and growth. It's also fun, empowering and expansive. It's the hear-me-roar, reclaim-your-life part of growing from trauma. And it's an awesome path to walk.

Traumatic conclusions and beliefs

During a traumatic experience, and later as we process what occurred, we each understand the threat, overwhelm and powerlessness differently. Unfortunately, most people draw negative conclusions about themselves and the world. There are many reasons for this type of negative appraisal. One reason is that the sense of threat pushes our thinking to some very dark places. Another reason has a lot to do with the support, validation and acknowledgement we received at the time. Many people, especially in childhood, experienced a lack of interest or dismissal of their feelings at the time of their trauma (e.g. *You're okay, don't worry about it, it wasn't that bad*). Others experienced more severe invalidation (*You're being ridiculous, grow up, stop overreacting*). Not having feelings validated can lead to children internalising their feelings. In a nutshell, this means that we presume something is wrong with us, that we're to blame, that our feelings are bad or wrong, and that we are bad or wrong. This type of invalidation is the beginning of low self-worth, shame and a whole host of negative beliefs about ourselves and the world.

Not all people who experience trauma develop low self-esteem and negative beliefs, however. Some miraculous people draw very positive conclusions. I'll tell you all about these people, and where we need your thinking to head, in chapter seven. For now, here are some common conclusions that people often draw from distressing and overwhelming experiences, whether they occur in childhood or in adulthood:

- I'm weak
- I'm useless
- I'm damaged
- I'm a victim
- I'm bad
- I can't do anything right
- I can't protect myself or others
- I can't stop bad things from happening
- People can't be trusted
- People are dangerous
- People hate me
- People are out to get me
- The world is dangerous
- It happened because of the sort of person I am
- It happened because of how I acted
- Nothing I do or say will ever change anything.

These conclusions are emotionally-led cognitive responses to an overwhelming threat and sense of powerlessness. I'm sure you've heard of them before. In the therapy or coaching world, they're referred to as self-limiting beliefs. Self-limiting beliefs are deeply held beliefs that need to be addressed and shifted before growth can continue. They're our blocks. They sit at the heart of our negative life repetitions and patterns.

I'm not suggesting that you're walking around thinking 'I'm damaged' or 'Nothing I do or say will ever change anything.' I'm suggesting that these beliefs are in your sub-conscious, driving your thinking, feelings and behaviour. They are more than just thoughts, they're deeply engrained beliefs that link to our self-concept, identity, feelings and life choices.

I'm mentioning these negative conclusions here for two reasons. First, I think it's useful to begin to consider how our past traumas have affected our beliefs about ourselves and the world around us. Second, I'm mentioning them because so many people I speak with don't realise that their negative self-beliefs are actually part of their traumatic reaction.

These kinds of beliefs aren't a sign of madness or permanent damage. These kinds of beliefs don't reflect an external reality. All these kinds of beliefs *mean* is that someone has unresolved trauma. Something happened to them – it may have been something big, but it could have been something everyday, something commonplace. If it happened before the age of five, they might not even remember it. Whatever it was, their adrenaline, overwhelm and powerlessness interfered with their ability to think. It was in this space that they drew negative, damaging, self-fulfilling conclusions about themselves and the world. They decided they're a failure. They decided they're a victim. They decided people couldn't be trusted.

You should know that these types of negative beliefs are such common responses to trauma that many of them are actually included on the list of diagnostic traumatic symptoms.[8] Take a moment to really feel what I've just said. That painful, untrue, self-limiting belief that you carry is not actually about *you* at all – it's a common response to trauma. In that one moment, your sense of threat, overwhelm and powerlessness drove your negative thinking. And not because you're a freak. You had a common human response to an overwhelming perceived threat: a traumatic reaction.

Imagine if we could change the conclusions we came to in those moments, when we were overwhelmed and threatened. Instead of taking the experience as proof that we're weak, imagine if we could take it as proof that we're strong. Not a victim, but a survivor. Not damaged, but whole. Not proof that the world is dangerous, but proof that traumatic experiences happen and we survive, perhaps even thrive. Imagine.

Big-T traumas

'Big-T trauma' is the name given to severe experiences we universally recognise as often being traumatic. Big-T traumas tend to be out of the ordinary (e.g. natural disasters) and are either socially unacceptable (e.g. rape) and/or collectively considered severe and distressing (e.g. war). These kinds of experiences expose us to actual or threatened death, serious injury or sexual violence. These experiences could have happened to us, or we may have witnessed them, personally or professionally (e.g. as a first responder, nurse, firefighter or medic). Or we may have learnt about these experiences happening to someone we love. Big-T traumas include:

- war
- severe childhood emotional, physical or sexual abuse
- severe neglect or abandonment
- experiencing or witnessing abuse
- experiencing or witnessing violence

- rape or sexual assault
- catastrophic injuries or illness
- natural disasters, including earthquakes, hurricanes, fires and floods
- stressful births for mothers and infants (I'd like to add for fathers too)
- bereavement
- serious accidents
- sudden violent or accidental death
- severe human suffering.[9]

This part, right here, is my least favourite bit of the book. I don't want to present a list of human atrocities that will upset and trigger people. But I have to include it because these big-T traumas are why many of you are here. Perhaps it will help if I mention that between 70 and 90 per cent of us experience a big-T trauma during our life.[10] Seventy to 90 per cent: that's most humans. As I said before, trauma is about all of us. Whatever your traumas are, you're not alone.

How did you feel as you read the list? What was going on in your body? It's natural to feel a little upset or uncomfortable when presented with a list of awful life events. But perhaps it was more than that: did you feel anxious? Did your heart pound, or did you feel spaced out (begin to dissociate)? Maybe it's hard to spot your physical sensations? That's also very common.

Learning about trauma involves learning to observe our reactions. Broadly recognising whether our reactions to things we read or experience are comfortable (nice, pleasant, light, expansive) or uncomfortable (unpleasant, tight, tense, unsafe, odd, icky) is a great place to start. This paves the way for our trigger work and learning to really feel and embody our feelings. We need to start now, at this end of the book, not wait until part three. So take a moment before you read on to be *in* your body. Notice what's going on. If there's an uncomfortable physical feeling or emotion, be with it if you can: sit with it, watch it. Even if you can just do this for one second longer than usual, that's a win.

Other-t traumas

Peter Levine's bestselling book *Waking the Tiger* was first published in 1997 and since then has been published multiple times in thirteen languages.[11] Levine's research and approach has fundamentally altered the way we understand trauma. The first part of my explanation of trauma (see pages 18 to 19) is drawn from his work and I use his somatic (body-led) approach at various points in the book. In his more recent book, *Healing Trauma*, he writes:

> Perhaps the most important thing I have learned about trauma is that people, especially children, can be overwhelmed by what we usually think of as common everyday events . . . Trauma does not have to stem from a major catastrophe.[12]

Many people in the field of trauma use the term 'little-t trauma' to describe the kinds of events Levine is referring to. These are common experiences that are often overlooked because they're erroneously considered 'just part of life'. I don't like the term *little-t trauma* as it implies that the experiences are unimportant and *little*. A truer term would be the-myriad-of-traumas-that-new-research-and-evidence-have-demonstrated-lead-to-trauma. But this is a little long, though, so we'll use *other-t traumas* instead of the stigma-inducing 'little-t' term. Other-t traumas include:

- extreme social isolation[13]
- routine medical procedures or operations
- everyday accidents, slips, falls or near misses
- minor automobile accidents
- divorce
- infidelity
- loss of a job
- a business going under
- financial ruin, or threat of financial ruin
- feeling unseen, unheard or unloved (especially relevant to children)
- bullying
- betrayal
- neglect (e.g. unmet needs, lack of self-care)
- abandonment or feeling abandoned
- social rejection
- extreme parental reactions or disapproval
- alcoholism or addiction in the home
- parental mental-health issues (including narcissism).

So, I'm using the term *other-t traumas* to describe *any* event that hasn't historically been recognised as traumatic. This list isn't exhaustive because *any* experience that results in a traumatic reaction is an other-t trauma. I hope you see your traumatic experiences here, but if you don't, that in no way means they aren't traumas. As I keep saying – only you can really know your traumas, because only you know your reaction. If you had a traumatic reaction, it was a trauma. The fact that it's not on this list means nothing.

Our definition of trauma doesn't differentiate between big-T traumas and other-t traumas. For this reason, we won't use these words much as we move forward. But for now, the distinction between big-T traumas (experiences that society acknowledges are traumatic) and other-t traumas (experiences that society doesn't tend to acknowledge are traumatic) is useful because it draws attention to the misinformation we've been operating under. It begins to draw our attention to experiences that we found threatening and overwhelming, maybe even disturbing, but that we denied and minimised.

We live in a fast-moving world, where near-misses and emotional overwhelm are not given the weight and space they deserve. Too often, traumatic reactions are not acknowledged, even by the individual who experiences it.

What comes to mind when I ask you to consider your *other-t traumas*, the more common, overlooked experiences that we all carry? Think of all the near-misses we experience or might have seen others experience over the years. Add to that the frightening medical procedures. Think of school bullies or the car accidents we drove past.

Think about the common childhood fear that we are not seen, heard or loved by our parents. The events that, most likely, were given no weight and no space. Maybe no one said to you, 'You seem scared, you're frightened and you're overwhelmed . . . what do you need?' What I want you to understand is that those times you felt in danger, extremely overwhelmed, frozen to the spot or abandoned may be part of your trauma history. They may be influencing how you feel; how you think; how you behave and react, today.

This is a good moment to warn you that as you do your work and consider your own traumas, people may try to undermine you. What do you mean your trip to hospital was traumatic? He was such a nice guy, why would you say the relationship was traumatic? Your dad loved you, there's no way any of it was traumatic. And on and on and on. Brace yourself and hold true to your growing knowledge and insight. If they don't know what a trauma *is*, they won't *get* it. And if they don't *get* it, their opinions are unlikely to be able to help you heal.

I would like to add that not everyone's difficult experiences are traumas. The experiences on either list are not *always* experienced as traumatic. As I keep saying, we all react differently to different experiences. For many, these experiences are difficult or hard, perhaps even frightening or disturbing, but not traumatic. Our reaction determines whether they are traumatic or whether they are not. As we learn more about traumatic reactions, and how they show up in our lives today, you'll know whether an experience was difficult or traumatic.

Grounding techniques

I meet a lot of people who have experienced trauma but who don't know how to ground themselves. Some of these people have been working with therapists for years, but they still haven't been adequately taught this critical aspect of growth and resilience. Grounding is discussed in chapter eight, but I'm going to talk about it here because it'll be useful as we move through the book. If you had a very uncomfortable reaction to the information I've covered in this chapter, it will be useful now.

Grounding techniques sound much more *woo woo* and spiritual than they actually are. Maybe we should come up with a new name for them?! Simply put, they're tools you can use to bring yourself back to the here and now. The basic idea is that they reconnect you to your body when for whatever reason (stress, a traumatic reaction, overwhelm, etc.) you have become disconnected from your *self* and the present moment. They help your body regulate and calm itself so that you can function. The idea is that you become firmly, securely, solidly, safely anchored in the here and now, rather than drifting away or becoming lost in a feeling, worry, sensation or memory.

Over time, our grounding response becomes an automatic, habitual reaction to being triggered and over-whelmed. This response intervenes in the triggered reaction to break the cycle of physical symptoms, feelings, thoughts and behaviours. This can and does work, if you commit. But it takes practice.

I've included some of my favourite grounding techniques on pages 41 and 42. These techniques are your basic trauma first-aid. They're simple, but life changing. Depending on your journey so far, some of you may already use these techniques. I hope many of you do.

The techniques can be broadly split into two categories: safety and reconnection, and discharging energy. It's best to use the safety and reconnection techniques first, then if you need to (e.g. if you feel giddy, anxious, a rush of energy, racing heart, etc.) you can use a technique to discharge the arousal energy. If you require a greater sense of connection and safety after you've discharged the energy, you can use one of the safety and reconnection techniques again.

As we move through the book, the techniques can be used if you have an *uncomfortable* triggered reaction so that you can remain present and engage with the content of the book. If we try to crash on without stabilising, it's impossible to be in the present moment. Our past trauma – our fear, overwhelm, powerlessness, and old *stuff* – will be reading the book and affecting our ability to connect with the material. Stabilising by grounding ourselves is critical to achieving clarity, freedom and growth.

We can only heal when we feel safe. We can only access our feelings when we feel safe. Ever wondered why so many people cry when they sing? It's because the songs make them feel safe and connect them to their bodies . . . and their feelings. The reverse of this is also true – when we feel unsafe, we can't access our feelings. We're rigid, anxious, in a state of paralysis and fear, disconnected from ourselves . . .

and our feelings. Some of you may often feel unsafe. I hear you. I felt like that for a very long time. I wanted to feel safe, but I also had huge subconscious resistance to feeling my feelings, as they were overwhelming and confusing. I subconsciously kept myself feeling unsafe (anxious, rigid, disconnected) so I didn't have to feel. This is the paradox of trauma. We want to recover and feel safe, but this involves us *feeling*. For many, staying in an unsafe state feels, paradoxically, more comfortable, than feeling safe (which brings with it all the old uncomfortable *shit*).

I wanted my feelings buried. I didn't want to go there, and if you'd presented me with a list of techniques to reconnect my mind with my body (and therefore *feel*), I would have struggled. Most likely some of you feel this way now. That's okay. Try the techniques – play with them, be open, be aware of your resistance, but don't push yourself too far. Watch what comes up.

If you connect with your body and you find that your fear increases, stop. If you connect with your body and the trauma symptoms increase, stop. At times I've needed the safety and security of working closely with a therapist to feel and be in my body. Some of you may need this too. That's really okay. Trauma recovery is slow and steady. As I said in the introduction, trauma healing is unique and belongs to us. Some of you may love the grounding techniques; for others it might be a step too far. Another of my favourite recovery phrases: *take what you want and leave the rest*. If you need to leave aspects of this mind–body connection for now, that's okay. You decide. You know best.

Grounding techniques
Safety and reconnection techniques

- Polyvagal breathing (4/8 rule):[13] Breathe deep into your belly for the count of four, and breathe out for the count of eight. Do this inhale/exhale at least four times, but ideally for up to three minutes. Modify the count if you need.
- Polyvagal breathing (voo): Take deep, slow, breaths into your stomach and as you breathe out, let out a deep, low, long 'Vooooooooo' sound coming up all the way from the depths of your belly. Focus fully on each breath. Take your time. Both types of polyvagal breathing (4/8 and voo) activate the vagus nerve and our para-sympathetic nervous system, which brings a sense of safety.[14]
- Out loud or in your mind, reconnect to your identity today (e.g. *I'm thirty-eight years old, I live in Australia, I have three children*) and remind yourself that your reaction is old (e.g. *My reaction is old, it's not about me today, today I am safe*).
- Look around you. What can you see? Say (ideally out loud) what you can see (e.g. *I can see a red notebook on my white desk. When I turn around, I can see a big tree outside my window.*) Keep going for as long as you need.
- As above, but what can you hear? (e.g. *I can hear a car go by. I can hear the downstairs tap running. I can hear a bird.*) Many find it comforting to close their eyes as they do this.
- Stand up and feel the pressure of your feet pushing into the ground. Focus on your feet – your energy will shift as your focus shifts. Feel the strength in your legs. Gently push one foot and then the next into the ground.

- Rub your hands together for a few seconds, then push the palms together. Really be with your hands, be aware of every sensation, the heat and the pressure.
- Cross your arms over your chest and give yourself a cuddle. Repeatedly squeeze the outside of your arms near your shoulders.
- Use affirmations. Ideally state them out loud with real strength and energy from your belly. Say them as many times as you need. Here are some of my favourites: *I am safe, I am grounded, I am solid, I am strong, I am healing, I am healthy, I am love.*
- Find a part of your body that feels okay. Even if it's just a small spot, notice that it feels safe, notice that it feels comfortable. Realigning and refocusing on the good feelings in our body is a big part of healing. For some it's their thumb, for others their calf muscle, for some it's their bum cheeks! Try to scout out a place that feels okay, pleasant even; notice, acknowledge the 'okay-ness' and stay there for a moment if you can.
- Meditate. Close your eyes and take some deep slow breaths into your belly, then breathe normally. Focus your attention on the centre of your heart space (picture a ball of golden light, or if you prefer, just notice the movement of your ribs). Or some prefer to say a mantra (perhaps one of the affirmations like *I am safe*) slowly, gently and repetitively in their mind.

Discharging energy
- Get up, walk around, run, stretch, wiggle your hips, move however you want and however feels good – let your body take the lead, shift your energy.
- Punch the air or a pillow.
- Sing or dance! With as much feeling and energy as you need!

Start with the technique you feel drawn to. Some days you might only need one technique; other days you may need to use many of them consecutively. Try combining one or two. Try changing bits that don't work for you. Do you feel safer with your eyes open or closed? Standing or sitting? These techniques are not set in stone, so play around with them. You'll know if they've worked because you'll gradually shift from being overwhelmed, anxious, afraid or disconnected back to the present moment and to yourself. You may need to do them repeatedly, and that's okay. Practise. The more you use them, the more your body will respond. But please remember, the idea is to feel less scared and less triggered – if a technique exacerbates your symptoms, stop.

New-t or old-t trauma?

Before we move on, I want to highlight something that I don't think is mentioned often enough as we collectively talk about trauma. Experiencing a previous trauma is a key predictor of experiencing another one.[15] In short, if you experience a trauma, say in childhood, you're more likely to experience a traumatic reaction to a difficult experience later in life.

Understanding that our nervous system is *overactive* after a traumatic experience is one way we can understand the link between childhood traumatic reactions and adult trauma. Our heightened sense of threat, for example, leads to more frequent perception of threats, opening the door to a traumatic reaction.

We can also understand the link when we think about triggered unprocessed memories. The sense of threat, over-whelm, powerlessness, emotions, sensations and beliefs that we experience during a traumatic experience as an adult can trigger old emotions, sensations and beliefs from our childhood traumas. The reaction itself (say, the sense of powerlessness) triggers the old unprocessed memory. So, our reaction to a big-T or other-t trauma that happens to us when we're an adult can be partly new and partly old.

I'm not saying that all adult traumatic reactions occur because the experience triggers an older trauma from child-hood. This is absolutely not the case. Our first trauma can occur in adulthood, of course. But in my experience, many people who experience trauma in adulthood realise along the way, as they do the work, that the recent adult trauma has been triggered by an older trauma from childhood. That's why most therapists are so keen on the whole 'What was your childhood like?' People hate it, but the truth is it's the feelings, trauma, experiences and beliefs that are buried in childhood that usually hold the key to real growth and change.

Chapter Two

Grey and messy

Chapter one gave you an explanation of trauma and some nice, neat categories for understanding it. Chapter one was black and white; chapter two is grey and messy. Here, I look at the stuff that makes us all uncomfortable. We're going to consider childhood trauma, attachment trauma (from your infant relationship with your parents), relational trauma (caused by relationships) and buried trauma (the stuff you can't remember). It's not nice and neat, and can be close to the bone, but it's critical that we 'go there' so we can get really clear about our own past.

Childhood trauma and denial

Childhood trauma just means trauma that happened during childhood. I've singled it out because it's extremely common, but many people pretend that it isn't. I've come to realise that we all have an odd 'anything goes, pretend it didn't happen, move on' brick wall around childhood. The first rule of *Fight Club* is also the first rule of childhood – don't talk about it. So when I ask an adult if they've ever been verbally abused, and they say 'No', I wait. Then, gently and respectfully, I enquire about their childhood. I might reframe the question: So, as a child there was no verbal abuse? The pretend-it-didn't-happen veil drops and they engage with their younger self. Yes, they say: Yes, there was.

We deny and minimise traumatic events from our child-hood. I get why we do it. It lets us carry on with the show. But if we want to grow, it's critical we stop minimising events that occurred when we were young. These events have left an imprint that has created different traumatic reactions and loops that still affect us today. It's uncomfort-able to own the fact that we carry childhood trauma, but it's important we do.

The difficulty with trauma – not just childhood trauma, but all trauma – is our denial. Admitting we've experienced something traumatic is, for many, half the battle. Things shift when we do. The word is frightening. People think that admit-ting something was traumatic is like admitting we can't cope. Many people think experiencing trauma happens because of weakness. They're wrong. It's not because of weakness or sensitivity. It's very human. It's protective.

If we can stop asking, 'What's wrong with me?' and instead ask, 'What did I react to?' our life takes a very different path. At a social level, if we could all stop asking,

'What's wrong with that person?' and instead ask, 'What's that person reacting to?' we'd all refocus on the real issue: trauma. I'm not alone in this desire to reframe trauma and mental health. You too can be part of the solution by considering a person's mental health today as a reaction to something that happened before.

Admitting something was – or is – traumatic means everyone has to look at their behaviour. Denying trauma absolves ourselves and everyone who was there at the time. It's much more comfortable for everyone involved if we just all keep up appearances. You'll save your mum a tonne of heartache if you never point out to her that her aggression, violence and verbal abuse was traumatic for you. If you don't call it trauma, your dad won't have to consider why he ignored what was happening. Your aunt, who could tell something wasn't right, won't have to consider her denial. If we don't call it trauma we can keep up appearances. We can keep pretending it was perfect. We can stay in control. We can avoid the pain of reality. Over the years I've heard versions of the stories below time and time again, both professionally as a researcher and personally on my own healing journey:

> 'My mum did drink a lot, loads actually, but she was also a lot of fun. There are a few times I remember not liking it – at parties and stuff when she was slurring her words or falling over a lot. It affected my brother much more than me. He seemed to take it really person-ally and he's never had alcohol actually. He got really wound up when she drank, but I was okay with it.'

'My mum was really distant. She was often sad or anxious. I just didn't know how to help. She had bad postnatal depression after my sister was born – I'm so sad for my sister about that. I remember a couple of holidays where mum had loads of energy, but more often I remember her kind of sitting and watching. She never yelled or anything, but we all tried our best not to upset her because we didn't want her to be sad or to worry. I guess it's sad, but I also feel really lucky I have such a good relationship with her.'

'My dad worked away from home, for months at a time. The house was really different when he came back for his month off. My sister and I were both scared of him in a way. Not that he was scary really, he just had a bad temper. He only hit me a couple of times and both times I was being really challenging. I remember winding him up deliberately. He used to suddenly flip out at me. I don't think he liked having kids around, but we get on better now I'm older.'

'I didn't really enjoy school. It was okay, but I found the other kids difficult. I had one good friend, but the other kids really didn't like me. I don't fully get why! I guess I was really annoying! Most of the time it was just saying mean stuff, silly kid stuff, or leaving me out. There were a couple of times they got nasty and hit me, but that was rare. School's difficult for so many kids – it's like a rite of passage!'

'My brother was hit by a car when I was younger. It was awful! He was on his bike on the pavement and fell into the road. I ran to try and stop him but couldn't reach him in time. The six weeks afterwards weren't nice as he was in intensive care and mum and dad were frightened he wouldn't make it. It's really affected them, I can tell. They are still very protective of him and since the accident have really focused on him, which I totally understand. I worry about them and him. I really try and look after them, even when I'm away at uni.'

'I remember this boy called Simon. I was probably about eight and he was maybe twelve. He used to stick his hand right down my pants on the school bus. I was so embarrassed, I just froze and went along with it. I remember feeling sick! I haven't actually told anyone that before, I'm really embarrassed I let him do it.'

Can you feel the denial hidden in these stories? It's an icky, sticky, jarring kind of feeling. It's that odd feeling you get when somebody says something that just doesn't *feel* right. I've heard many different versions of these childhood traumas and they all have the same energy around them. In all the meetings I've attended and groups I've facilitated, there are people (usually people having a really hard time) denying the painful experiences they had as a child. They tell a story like the ones above and they know, and I know, and anyone else listening knows, that things aren't right. That the experience they're describing is not okay or insignificant. What we're all thinking is: 'That sounds really awful and you look a lot like someone having a really difficult time . . . surely that's not a coincidence.'

So why, even when things aren't going well for us, do we deny that our childhood experiences may have something to do with our problems? Although it's a lot easier for us and our families if we don't go there, it's also about something deeper. Millions have watched Brené Brown's shame and vulnerability TED talk. Her work and her storytelling are awesome.[1] But I want you to know that before shame often comes . . . what? Can you guess? Trauma. Shame is a common reaction to a traumatic experience. So what are we ashamed of? Those questions are very personal, but in the examples above, what would be your best guess? What do you think these people are ashamed of?

I think each and every one of these people is probably embarrassed by how they were treated. I think they believe they would not have been treated this way if they were more loveable. They carry the shame of being treated very badly by someone who should have loved and respected them. A mother drinking, a mum with depression, a father hitting, a school not dealing with bullying, parents prioritising one child over another, and an older, more powerful person taking advantage of someone vulnerable. The tellers of these stories deserved better. But still, they won't call these incidents what they were, because they're ashamed. Do you know why I know these incidents are all trauma?

Because if they weren't, each of these people would own it. They'd say, 'This older boy touched me up, what a prick.' It wouldn't be hidden. There wouldn't be excuses or embarrassment. There wouldn't be shame.

Attachment trauma

Some of the childhood experiences I've mentioned above are caused by external 'events' (e.g. car accidents), but if you look closely you'll notice that most of the experiences are interpersonal or 'relational', meaning that they involve human relationships. Attachment trauma is a specific type of relational trauma that refers to the trauma experienced by an infant or a very young child within an emotionally or physically neglectful, or abusive, parental relationship.

Attachment refers to the connection between a baby or young child and their parents or primary carers. A healthy emotional bond between a child and their parent develops as the relationship develops. The adult and the child need to be emotionally in tune with each other. If the child looks sad, the parent needs to see the sadness and respond. If the parent is annoyed, the child needs to understand this. This emotional in-tune-ness *is* the connection, which is the attachment bond. Within these first relationships, we learn to regulate our feelings (i.e. we learn to differentiate, understand and control feelings). We learn who we are and who we are in relation to others. We learn that our feelings matter, and that we matter. We learn how valued we are. We learn our worth.

51

The outcome of consistent parental care, affection and attention is a *secure* attachment bond. The child feels secure in the relationship and secure in themselves. They know where they stand, know they can rely on their parent and know they're loved and loveable. The child feels they are seen and heard. A securely attached child has a meaningful, consistent, loving reference point from which they can develop an integrated sense of self. Sounds nice, doesn't it?

If a child is emotionally neglected, and their parent isn't emotionally in tune with them, things don't go so well. They develop an *insecure* attachment bond rather than a secure one. So instead of feeling secure in themselves and the relationship, they feel insecure about themselves and the relationship. They do not feel they can rely on their parent, and do not feel loved or loveable. They may feel like they fade into the background, their feelings ignored or discounted. The child doesn't feel seen or heard in an authentic way. Instead of self-worth, they develop feelings of worthlessness. Instead of feeling valued, they feel of no value to those they love. They may develop a fragmented sense of self – meaning that they have a weak identity and are unclear about who they are, particularly in relationships with others. Insecure attachment is about how we feel about ourselves, and ourselves in relation to others.

Young children can experience insecure parental attachments as traumatic. We call it attachment trauma, but really, it's no different to any other trauma. An infant or young child is totally dependent on the adults in their lives.

Because of this complete dependence (they'll literally die if their parent won't care for them), the threat is perceived as large and therefore very overwhelming. By definition, infants and young kids are completely powerless to change their situation – they are helpless. Think of our equation back in chapter one. A child perceives a threat (that their parents can't or won't meet their need for sustenance, attention and/or love), and is overwhelmed by the magnitude of the threat and their own helplessness. Perceived threat + overwhelm + powerlessness = trauma. I've singled out this type of trauma because it's relevant to so many, but really, it's just trauma.

The outcome of inadequate, traumatic first relationships is far-reaching. These first attachment relationships become blueprints for all subsequent relationships. They guide what we expect from others and how we view ourselves in relation to others. That's great if your attachment pattern is secure; not so great if there's trauma and insecurity there. We think we *know* what we mean when we describe someone as secure or insecure. We use these terms a lot, right? Well, they stem from attachment research and theory. An insecure adult is playing out the relationship patterns, fears and dysfunctions learnt as an infant.

Relational trauma

Attachment trauma is a type of *relational* trauma – a type of trauma that develops from being in a long-term, highly stressful, complex, difficult, neglectful or abusive relationship.

Most often, 'relational trauma' refers to relationships before adulthood, but some abusive adult relationships are referred to as relational trauma. I'm mentioning this type of trauma because attachment trauma isn't the whole story. Child maltreatment, sexual abuse, sexual harassment, rape, psychological and emotional abuse, bullying, domestic violence, narcissistic abuse, abandonment, emotional enmeshment (i.e. unclear personal boundaries within family relationships), rejection, complex grief, traumatic loss and other forms of attachment betrayal or disruption[2] are types of relational trauma.

Relational trauma involves a 'profound violation of the human connection'.[3] If a parent is involved, the attachment bond will be severely impaired, but relational trauma is broader than attachment trauma. It's about all human relationships. It's about trust, safety and connection. Or rather, it's about the breaking of these things.

Instead of going too heavily into detail about relational trauma, I'm going to tell you about Max. I met Max when I was about twenty-seven at a retreat centre.

He hadn't been on this type of retreat before, so he was a little overawed. He was quiet and withdrawn, like he was there as an observer rather than as a participant. On the second day we dived straight into the hard stuff – childhood trauma and shame. It was part discussion and processing, part clearing and releasing. The main message shared was that healthy shame and toxic shame are radically different, and the toxic shame we carry always belongs to someone else – we were handed it.

Max told the group about his volatile relationship with his father, who was a textbook narcissist. Max's dad had a job that meant he travelled a lot, and when he was at home, he was either drinking with his friends or angrily locked away in his study. He was arrogant and completely wrapped up in himself. So, obviously, he paid little attention to Max's needs and consistently disregarded his feelings. His dad was either cruel (not a word Max used), absent or an over-the-top drunk. The word that came up time and time again in Max's description of his childhood was – *confusing*.

As an adult, Max was completely burnt out at work. He'd met a girl and, now that he was looking to the future, he was worried he was going to become a workaholic like his father. He was also deeply afraid of losing his girlfriend. He couldn't 'do' relationships. Whether the relationship was with a partner or a friend, he found it extremely overwhelming and confusing.

The thing that really stood out about Max was that he said he had no bad feelings towards his father. Max blamed himself completely for the poor relationship. I mean, he didn't say that, but we all heard it. He said what hard work he was as a kid, how he'd been too needy. He said he was a pretty dull kid, so to a man like his dad, who was so smart and funny, he must have been unbearable to be around. You know those moments where you feel the inconsistency? When you just know that the words coming out of someone's mouth aren't their truth? Well, that's what it felt like to hear Max say he thought his dad was a stand-up guy. It didn't ring true. I believe in the power of forgiveness and letting go – these are critical parts of my own healing – but Max hadn't forgiven his father; he was denying there was a problem in the first place.

Max came to the retreat with a gnawing sense that things weren't as they should be. His intuition and instinct got him there, despite his outward denial. Over the four days, he moved from denial – of his anger towards his dad, his relational trauma and shame – to acceptance. He joined the dots, realising that his chronic overworking was driven by his fear of failure. His chronic relationship fears were driven by his fear of abandonment; his denial, shame, overwhelm and confusion were driven by the relational trauma itself.

He left the retreat exhausted and sad, yes. But more importantly, he also left hopeful, honest, empowered and connected to himself and his reality. This last word – reality – is important. Relational trauma is crazy-making. It makes us double back on ourselves, question our instincts, feelings, thoughts and even ourselves. Max had been living in a murky, confusing family system as a child. It was a bewildering mix of parental narcissism, emotional abandonment and shame. He was told one thing, but observed another. He expressed a feeling, and was told he was wrong. He couldn't see the wood for the trees. But at the retreat, Max stepped into himself. He owned *his* past and *his* present. He called it trauma. He said *enough*, and he took his life back.

Buried trauma

Buried trauma refers to traumatic experiences we can't remember. Instead of a clear memory, we may have snippets of a memory. Perhaps there's one striking image or scene that comes to us in our dreams. Perhaps an image pops up at very odd times – when you smell a certain aroma or are in a particular type of house. Perhaps it's a collection of random thoughts, images, feelings or sensations that make little sense. Either way, these snippets don't bring a sense of joy – they often bring a sense of dread.

Perhaps there's no image at all, just a blank space where memories should be? Or maybe there's an overwhelming sense of fear or helplessness? Or perhaps you're stuck in shame, but don't know why? Perhaps, instead of fear or shame, it's anger? I could go on and on and on. And on. What I'm getting at is at the heart of this book: if you have a negative feeling, sensation or thought which occurs repeatedly and with great strength, it could stem from trauma. It could be part of your traumatic reaction.

These unexplained experiences are profoundly confusing and far more common than anyone wants to admit. What we're looking for are patterns in your triggered emotions, sensations and cognitions. The thing you're stuck in, that's on repeat, will lead you back to the trauma – it gives you an idea of what has been buried. What I'm saying is, just because you can't remember a specific traumatic experience, it doesn't mean there isn't one. If there's a traumatic reaction, there's a trauma.

There are a few different types of traumatic experiences that commonly end up buried and hidden. One is pretty obvious. We can't remember events that happened before the age of three years old. And new research actually puts this age of amnesia nearer to seven years old for many people.[4] So, no matter the experience, if it happened when you were very young, you're highly unlikely to remember it.

Take a little moment here to remember the section on attachment. Attachment bonds typically develop before the age of three. You're unlikely to remember what it was like when you were a baby – the relationship is buried. If there was a relational or, specifically, an attachment trauma, it's buried. It's buried, but you had a reaction that you still carry. It affects your body, your mind, your relationships, your health and your work. Whether it was emotional trauma or physical trauma, if it happened when you were young, you feel it. You carry it and you live with it, but *it* is buried.

There's another type of traumatic experience that is, by definition, buried. Intergenerational trauma can be passed on to us by our parents, our grandparents and our ancestors. Within psychology and neuroscience there's increasing evidence that we carry the trauma of those who went before us.[5] Emotional learning and social conditioning is one way to explain the association. So, if your mother, father or carer experienced a severe trauma, this can be passed on to you through similar mechanisms as were described in the attachment trauma section. As a traumatised parent tries to parent, their trauma interferes with how they interact with their child.[6]

Even more incredible than the idea of intergenerational socialised trauma is epigenetic trauma, where experiences in someone's lifetime can actually change the way their DNA is expressed. If you're a science nerd, you know all about epigenetics. If you're like the rest of us, here's a basic explanation:

Epigenetics literally means *on top of* genetics.[7] It refers to the part of our DNA that's modified by certain external factors (e.g. diet, sleep). Tiny chemical tags are added to or removed from our DNA in response to the environment we're living in. These tags turn genes on or off, allowing humans to adapt to certain environmental conditions without affecting their legacy DNA. The genetic DNA sequence doesn't change, but the *expression* of the DNA does. We are handed our DNA at birth, but our environment interacts with it to produce *us*. Until fairly recently, we thought all this epigenetic stuff was reprogrammed when a woman produces an egg and a man produces sperm. We thought each generation got a fresh chance to make the most of the genetic code their family had passed to them. But we now know that some of the epigenetic layer is passed on to us. The implications of this are huge. Your parents' experiences during their lifetime can have a very real impact on you, your children and generations to come. There's increasing evidence that traumatic experiences can affect this epigenetic layer and be handed down. Human studies have found traumatic physiological and psychological traits passing from one generation to another. Animal studies suggest that even fear and threat-specific sensitivity can be passed down.[8]

Whether we're considering experiences from when we're very young, how our parents raised us, or our inherited trauma, I hope this section convinces you that trauma can be, and very often is, buried. The outcome of buried trauma is an individual who is extremely confused because they *carry* trauma, but who has no memory on which to pin their symptoms. Their body and their emotions are telling them there's trauma, but there's no experience they can remember to help them find meaning. They can't understand the trauma in any meaningful way, so confusion and shame is added to confusion and shame.

Here, I could tell you about so many different people I've met along the way. People who have buried relational trauma or just plain buried trauma. So many people come to mind, because so much trauma is buried. There are even aspects of my own story I could describe. But I'm going to tell you about Sam because hearing her story, many years ago, changed me. I contemplated her and her life, and what her experiences meant not just for her but for all of us. Sam helped me understand trauma and the damage it can cause, in a very deep way.

I met Sam when I was working in a rehab centre, facilitating support groups. Sam, who was forty-two at the time, had just been admitted for alcohol abuse and clinical depression. She was charming and witty, and I warmed to her immediately. After one of the group sessions, as I was walking down the corridor past the bedrooms, I heard a shout: 'Hello Miss Sarah, nice boots!' It was Sam, peering round the door as she lay on her bed. With a smile I said:

'Why thank you, Miss Sam.' She asked me to come and sit with her, which I did. We talked about the group and I asked her how she was finding it.

'I feel like I could say anything and wouldn't be judged – which isn't something I'm used to,' she said.

Sam told me she was realising that she'd never really been honest, with other people or herself. She explained that she didn't think she had clinical depression but that she had 'clinical shame'. Sam described how she'd lived her whole life with this hidden, painful sense that she'd done something terrible and wrong when she was a kid. She told me that deep down she'd always felt disgusting and that she'd worked really hard to make sure no one realised just how gross and rotten she really was.

Sam said that sometimes these feelings were so intense, she would self-harm. She described her bouts of depression, despair and suicidal thoughts, and how over the past year it felt like she was losing her mind, 'for real'. She drank every day, not because she wanted to, but because it was the only thing that stopped the panic, anxiety and fear.

Almost as an afterthought, Sam said, 'And none of it makes any sense, because nothing has happened to me. Some people go through really bad shit, but all I've got are these weird dreams about the neighbour's house. And maybe something happened, but most likely I'm just a freak.'

I sat with Sam, quietly witnessing her story, until someone knocked on the door reminding her the next group was about to start. As Sam rushed off, I walked to the staffroom thinking about her pain and confusion. I was there with her, also wondering why she (or any of us) ended up with so much shame and self-loathing. I pulled out Sam's file, looking for her treatment plan. At the end of the notes, her psychologist had written:

'Intrusive traumatic memories related to childhood neighbour's house. Request EMDR.'

This short clinical note spoke volumes to me. I understood that Sam had most likely experienced a trauma when she was very young, but that she couldn't fully remember it. Part of her knew something had happened to her, but she had no clear memory, so she'd been living in a confused limbo of shame, fear and self-doubt. What she described – her panic, anxiety, shame, low self-esteem, self-harm, drinking and low mood – was part of her traumatic reaction. In that moment I understood that trauma can lurk in the background, make us question our sanity and worth, and quietly fuel our self-destruction.

As Sam worked with different therapists, she remembered more from her childhood. Not everything, but enough for her to understand that she'd been repeatedly molested by her neighbour when she was very young. She realised her current pain was a reaction to her past. As Sam did her work, she stopped running shamefully away from her deepest fears (*something happened to me, I'm broken*) and stood still to face her truth. By the time Sam left the treatment centre six months later, her confusion and self-doubt had been replaced with clarity, and this clarity was her path to freedom.

Chapter Three

What's a traumatic reaction?

In many ways, I'm not going to introduce anything radically new to our explanation of trauma in this chapter. Why? Because a trauma is defined by our traumatic reaction. So, in chapter one, as I defined trauma I was, of course, defining traumatic reactions. Overwhelm, powerlessness, fight, flight, freeze, traumatic beliefs and unprocessed memories. These are all elements of what a trauma is *and* are all traumatic reactions. Our trauma is our reaction; our reaction is our trauma.

This chapter adds detail. We'll distinguish between the core reactions and other, more unusual, ones. We'll consider disconnection from self, our unbreakable core, the Trauma Loop, triggering, stress and PTSD in more detail. By the end of this chapter, you're going to be a trauma expert too.

You're not broken

You've been through a lot in your life. You've had some difficult experiences. Some of these experiences may have been traumatic. But hear this: there's nothing *wrong* with you.

There's an unbreakable centre in all of us, sitting underneath all our reactions. It sits under your thinking and behaviour, under your ego and external identity. Some of you reading this will have been given a diagnosis before. Perhaps you've been told you have depression, or anxiety. Perhaps some of you have PTSD. I need to be very clear that I am not disputing the diagnoses. What I'm disputing is the idea that there's anything *wrong* with you – there isn't. At the core of you is something strong and beautiful.

Traumatic reactions disconnect us from the parts of ourselves that are supposed to take the lead in creating our lives. They disconnect us from our unbreakable core – the beautiful, universal, essential part of each of us. They separate us from our wisest, instinctual higher self, and from our worth, our purpose and our sense of belonging. They detach us from our sense of identity; from our under-standing of who we are and why we're here. They uncouple us from our body and from the much-needed sense of presence and grounding that our body provides. They also disconnect us from our social self and our understanding of who we are in relation to other people. Our entire being can feel fragile, dispersed and out of reach.

Whether your disconnection feels minor and surmount-able, or severe and insurmountable, we all need to contemplate the idea of self. We all need to consider how our past pain may have falsely made us believe that we're broken, when in reality what we're dealing with is disconnection. The connection to self needs to be mended, but *you* don't.

I'd like to tell you a story. I've done all sorts of yoga over the years, but it's Sivananda yoga that really resonates with me. When I lived in West London I use to go to the Siva-nanda centre in Putney. There was something about the people, the energy and the movements that made my heart sing. About ten years ago, I decided to spend some time at the Sivananda ashram in France. It had been a dream of mine for a long time, so I was excited and a little appre-hensive as I stepped onto the train that would whisk me to Paris, and then onto the ashram.

The ashram was one of the most healing places I have ever visited. As soon as I stepped into the space, I was met with peace and acceptance. Somehow, everyone under-stood that their egos and external identities were to be left at the door. I felt like I entered the space naked and free. It was calming and incredibly powerful.

Every morning at 4.30 a bell rang and, in silence, we all softly made our way to the meditation space – a huge room in the rooftop eaves of the centre, with a vast window at one end. We meditated and chanted until sunrise, eyes closed, at peace and as one. I cannot fully explain the joy and calm that I felt. On the morning of the last day I walked to the meditation room early, sat on my beautiful orange cushion and began to meditate as others slowly entered the room in silence. I was gently focusing on my heart and mentally chanting the mantra *Om namo narayanaya*, loosely translated as *I honour the divine universal energy within all*. I repeated this phrase hundreds of times, rhythmically, and as I did so I became aware of a ball of energy in my chest. It was orangey-yellow in colour and was as bright and warming as the sun. As the rhythm of the mantra ebbed and flowed, so too did this ball of light – as if it was living and breathing. I cannot fully convey its beauty. There was a presence to it that was mesmerising. I had *imagined* things before, *visualised* things before, but this was different. It felt like nothing I'd ever experienced before. I heard laughter and joy. I felt deep and indescribable peace, and a knowing that has never left me. I knew that I had nothing to fear – that I was not broken – I just had to find ways to connect with this central, strong, essential core part of me. I sat with this *new* part of me for hours. I then gently opened my eyes and watched the sunrise through the expanse of window in front of me. I knew I would never be the same, and I wasn't. This profound experience directed my healing, just as it directs my words now. Unexpectedly, I'm starting to well up as I write this. Of all the information I've given you, this is the part that feels the most intimate.

Within this book I call this our *unbreakable core*. Some call it *soul*, others call it *spirit*, *God, essential self* or *higher self*. *Heart, divine spark, life force, essential nature, psyche, love, life-giving energy* – all terms humans have used to try to describe the indescribable life force within the body. A force so powerful that it sustains all life and holds every single atom together. Whether you see this force as natural or divine, it's real. And it connects you to everyone and everything around you. Whatever you want to call it and however disconnected you feel from it, it's there, I promise you. If it wasn't, you wouldn't be alive. If you have a heartbeat, you have this gentle, strong, healing, life-giving energy. It's your peace, your strength and your future. It *is* the present moment – existing in the breath and the space between thoughts. It's the energy that holds everything together. It's your home. And unlike your body and your external identity, unlike all those reactions, this essential part of yourself will never change. No matter how old you are or what kind of day you're having, when you connect to this aspect of your being it will always be just as it was and just as it always will be. Unlike so much in our lives, this core, and the energy that flows into it and from it, is completely reliable, predictable, accepting and loving. Play around, find whatever words feel natural and comfortable for you. Call it love, call it soul, call it energy, call it peace, call it God, call it light. It doesn't matter what word you use, it just matters that you find a space inside you that feels strong, whole and healing.

As you begin to consider your own traumatic reactions, I want you to try (really try) to keep hold of this idea – that there's a central part of you that's completely unbreakable. Your reactions have disconnected you from it, but it's still there. In fact, no matter how far away you walk from it, it's not going anywhere. Your reactions are the outside. The inside is golden.

The Trauma Loop explained

The Trauma Loop consists of one long chain of reactions that feed into each other, and gradually disconnect us from *us*. On the next page is a bare-bones illustration of what I'm getting at, and below that is a narrative explanation. I'm hoping that, between these two explanations, you'll find clarity and a firm understanding.

Threat

We perceive a threat. It might be the original trauma, or it might be something that reminds us of the original trauma – a trigger.

Survival response

The perceived threat sets off our survival response: fight or flight. This is an automatic, instinctive threat-response that's triggered by a part of our brain called the amygdala and sets off a cascade of neural and hormonal changes in our brain and body. These changes – which include flooding our body with adrenaline and other arousal hormones – happen within milliseconds. They're our body's way of preparing us to respond to the threat by either fighting or running for our lives (flight).

Polyvagal theory suggests that if our system becomes too aroused, a large central nerve within our parasympathetic

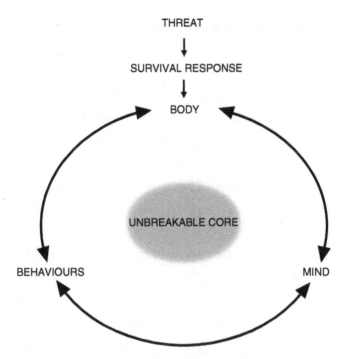

The Trauma Loop is a cycle of physical, emotional, cognitive and behavioural reactions fuelled by the survival (fight, flight, freeze) response to threat. These reactions feed into each other, often heightening each other's intensity. This loop of reactions prevents us from connecting with our unbreakable core – the essential part of our being that exists in the present moment.

nervous system – the vagus nerve – will shut down the entire system and we'll go into the third type of survival response: freeze.[1] Children are especially prone to the freeze response, which slams the brakes on the arousal hormones so we can play dead and hide.

The survival response can be momentary, but can continue indefinitely.

For more information, please see the glossary on page 228.

Body – physiological and emotional reactions

We experience the survival response as physical and emotional *symptoms*. This is an important point. Your survival response and your physical and emotional reactions are one and the same thing. Dissociation (feeling spaced out) is a *physical* manifestation of the survival response. Having a racing heart is a *physical* manifestation of the survival response. Fear is an *emotional* manifestation of the survival response. Anxiety is an *emotional* manifestation of the survival response. They're one and the same – *felt* aspects of the survival response, powered by all those arousal hormones and/or the vagus nerve shutdown response.

In fact, most traumatic reactions – whether they're physical, emotional or cognitive – are manifestations of the nervous system response and the arousal or shutdown hormones that have flooded our body.

Physical reactions include a racing heart, sweating, tense muscles, dissociation and feeling totally spaced out, being on guard, being easily startled, or feeling physically numb. Emotional reactions like fear, anxiety, shame, powerlessness, helplessness, overwhelm, anger, sadness and emotional withdrawal are also experienced in our body (although we become aware of them with the mind, and the emotion affects our thoughts).

These physical and emotional reactions can be instant (meaning they happen immediately, in real-time, along with the survival response) or they can become apparent as time goes on.

Notice that I have grouped emotions and physical sensations together in this section because, essentially, they're one and the same. Physical trauma symptoms are aspects of our emotions and vice versa. Differentiating between physical symptoms and our emotions is unhelpful. Physical reactions (e.g. tense muscles) instantly cue an emotional reaction (e.g. fear), and our emotional reactions instantly cue our physical reactions. We must learn to see them as intrinsically linked – two sides of the same coin. This is why somatic (body-led) approaches to trauma healing work so well. As practitioners work with the body they rebalance the nervous system, and help us discharge our physical tension and trapped emotions.

Mind – cognitive reactions

We think about, appraise and analyse the threat and our physical and emotional reactions in a *traumatic* way. What do I mean? During a traumatic reaction, our thinking is not balanced, grounded or rational. There's no fact-checking or useful analysis. It's traumatic thinking, driven by the flood of hormones that accompanies our survival response. We cognitively *react* to everything we're experiencing and feeling from within our sense of threat.

Like our body, our brain is flooded with hormones during a traumatic reaction. This affects our memory processes and our thought processes during and after the experience. Our conscious and subconscious cognitive processes go awry. Many people experience cognitive reactions such as confusion. We can't think straight, but we still do (think, that

71

is). And therein lies the danger. If we were able to say to ourselves – *I am having a traumatic reaction, so I must wait until I feel safe before I trust my thoughts* – then I suspect we'd all fare better. But obviously, we don't do that. We take each and every cognition and appraisal we experience as fact, just as we always do. We don't ask, '*Is it true?*' as the wonderful Byron Katie asks us to.[2] Our thoughts are racing, our thinking is extremely negative, yet still we most often just accept the conclusions we come to. We call ourselves failures. We tell ourselves we are to blame. It goes without saying (but I'll say it anyway) that this kind of traumatic thinking heightens physical and emotional reactions. Of course, if you tell yourself you're a failure and that you're to blame, your fear and shame is going to get worse, not better.

Our traumatic thinking, coupled with our emotional and physical reactions, leads to the development of subconscious traumatic beliefs. I'm referring to the silent, damaging conclusions we come to about ourselves and the world. Beliefs I've mentioned before, such as *I'm bad, I'm damaged, other people can't be trusted, I'm not capable, I'll never amount to anything, I'm unsafe*. These beliefs operate in a very underhand way throughout our life. They're easily triggered, but unlike many of the other more obvious reactions (e.g. anxiety) we're often unaware that these damaging beliefs are directing our behaviours.

To clarify, 'mind' includes three different types of cognitive reactions. *Conscious* traumatic thinking (e.g. repetitive negative thinking, extreme negative thoughts about ourselves and the world); the development of *subconscious* traumatic beliefs (e.g. *I'm worthless, I'm nothing, the world is unsafe, people can't be trusted*); and other cognitive symptoms (e.g. images or memories popping in to mind unexpectedly, confusion, difficulty concentrating, brain fog).

Behavioural reactions

So, there are all the physical and emotional reactions to the threat. Then, running alongside them and often making them worse, are the cognitive reactions. Now to the behavioural reactions. We react to the physical and emotional symptoms and the traumatic thinking by employing different strategies and techniques. These are the things we do to try and cope with what we're experiencing.

Many of us avoid. We bury the feelings, avoid the thoughts, avoid conversations about what's going on, avoid other people, avoid anything at all that might make us feel worse (or feel at all). Drinking alcohol, compulsive distraction (e.g. watching TV or checking your phone), compulsive busyness (e.g. tidying, making plans), over-eating and binging, under-eating, compulsive spending, risky sexual behaviour, self-harm, avoiding intimacy and touch, drug use and watching porn are some of the well-known types of traumatic coping. See chapter five for more detail.

Some of us people-please, or desperately seek approval and attention in the wrong places. This type of behaviour is increasingly acknowledged as a unique type of survival response called *fawn*.[3] It's characterised by co-dependency, lack of emotional boundaries, extreme self-sacrifice and ignoring one's own needs or wishes in favour of keeping others happy, interested and invested in the relationship. More correctly then, we would use the term 'fight, flight, freeze, fawn' – the four Fs. People-pleasing behaviour is still a way to avoid the pain of our own feelings, but it manifests in anxious behaviour focused on pleasing others rather than avoiding or confronting others.

Whichever traumatic coping strategy we employ, it locks us into a maladaptive cycle. Instead of discharging and calming the survival response, the strategies often prolong and exacerbate it. The behaviours and strategies might bring us temporary relief, but the physical, emotional and cognitive reactions will always return because nothing within the system has been rebalanced. In actual fact, all we've done is further cement the unbalanced, old neural pathways. The initial survival response is not discharged and we're stuck in a self-defeating, maladaptive loop.

Traumatic coping includes any dysfunctional behavioural strategy we use to cope with the physical reactions, emotions and cognitions. This does not, then, include healthy coping (e.g. talking, journalling, grounding, therapy, yoga). Dysfunctional coping keeps us trapped in the Trauma Loop. Healthy coping helps break free.

As well as traumatic coping, another part of this behavioural category is called *life patterns*. These patterns are the result of being trapped in the Trauma Loop over time. They're our long-term behavioural reactions to a lifetime of uncomfortable feelings, traumatic thinking patterns, subconscious traumatic beliefs and maladaptive coping strategies. They're patterns like repetitive conflict, broken relationships, abusive relationships, under-earning and self-sabotage. Just like everything else included here, these outcomes and patterns should be viewed as reactions. And just like everything else I've covered, they keep you trapped within the loop.

Unbreakable core

The Trauma Loop I've described disconnects us from ourselves and the present moment. We are connected solely to *old* reactions and to the past. We disconnect from three main parts of ourselves: our body, our unbreakable core (the wisest, instinctive, essential part of our being) and our adult self.

Over time, the physical, emotional, cognitive and behavioural reactions lead to a sense of disconnection from our body. Our body doesn't feel as if it belongs to us because we're constantly thrown into old, uncomfortable sensations. Being in our body – with all those difficult sensations, feelings and memories – is extremely painful, so we do what we can to not be *in* our body. In fact, many trauma symptoms serve this very purpose: to keep us out of, and away from, the pain. Think about dissociation, anxiety or repetitive thinking – these mechanisms serve to separate us from our body and the painful unprocessed memories that are surfacing.

This disconnection from our physical being is a spiritual disconnection too. Of course, the body is where our essential self resides. So, as we turn away from our body, we turn away from the stable, reliable, unchanging strength of our essential self. We *react to life* from within our traumatic disconnected state, rather than *act on life* from a place of core connection. The painful result of this separation is that we feel lost, unsure of who we are and why we're here. This spiritual disconnect can feel extremely lonely, leading us to despair and a sense of grief and loss.

In the moment, our triggered traumatic reactions lead to a disconnection from our adult self. We're thrown back to our child self, and the age we were when the painful traumatic experience happened. Over time, the process of disconnecting from our adult self and being thrown backwards to a younger consciousness deepens our sense of not knowing who we really are. Many of us struggle to grow and learn – to evolve – because we're constantly interrupted, constantly pulled backwards. As we begin to consider how, why and when we disconnect from our adult self, many of us realise that we spend much of life living from within our child consciousness. At work, at home, during intimate moments, as we try and lead, as we parent – our wounded younger self is often present and reacting.

As we break free from the Trauma Loop and all those external reactions, we reconnect to our body, to our unbreakable core and to our adult self. And as we reconnect to the essential part of ourselves, we're able to access our purpose, our wisdom, our instinct and our hope. These gifts allow us to strengthen our adult self. We become authentic and empowered. We're able to guide ourselves, hold ourselves, comfort ourselves and *know* the way forward.

The *other* reactions

Many of the common, uniform, traumatic symptoms that are well known and consistently appear as a response to a traumatic experience are mentioned above (e.g. feeling on guard, avoiding people, intrusive negative beliefs or images). A comprehensive list is included in the Appendix, on page 223. I've included this list of symptoms because I hope they'll help you better understand your own traumatic reactions. But these kinds of lists aren't how I came to know my trauma.

Here's how I realised I carry trauma: I sat in loving, open, safe spaces with other women and men, and I heard their stories. I heard them call out their past traumas and their current daily dysfunctions. I heard them voice their shame and their brutal negative thinking. I heard them describe their anger, fear and unrelenting sense of threat. They spoke about the many ways they tried to avoid feeling, thinking and being. They told story after story of a past fraught with childhood trauma, pain and stress. They saw their past trauma and their ongoing reactions to this trauma. I saw them join the dots and then *I* joined the dots for myself.

I also saw, as clear as day, that traumatic reactions are broad, unique and can be unusual. Think for a moment about the information I included in the introduction. Trauma is the gateway. It's anxiety and depression. It's diabetes and gastro issues. It's alcoholism and addiction. It's eating disorders. It's chronic back pain. It's . . . well, you get the gist, take a look at page 6 again and you'll see all the many human dysfunctions that are associated with trauma.

Actually, please don't get bogged down in a list; the whole point is that *you* decide what your trauma is. You decide its impact. You begin to observe and recognise your unique reactions.

Below are some of the unique, ongoing and pervasive reactions people attribute to their traumas. Some of these are physiological sensations, some are emotional. Some are traumatic thinking, others are traumatic coping. Some are instant reactions, others come later – they're outcome reactions (the outcome of living with instant reactions over a long period of time). Whatever they are, they're part of a person's unique Trauma Loop. They're part of the imprint of their trauma.

Get ready for the list of a lifetime. It's epic, and deliberately so. I'm trying to help you see just how diverse, broad and insidious traumatic reactions are in the real world. The fear, overwhelm and powerlessness can take us anywhere in terms of our mental and physical health. The reactions are grouped into three categories – body, mind and behaviours – based on where the reaction originates or is primarily experienced. I'm grateful to all who have shared these with me over the years.

Traumatic reactions
Body
The knot in my stomach when I see my dad
Narcolepsy
Obesity
The seizures I experience if I try to talk about what
    happened

What's a traumatic reaction?

Fibromyalgia
Overwhelm and anxiety when I see the Instagram icon
Shame if someone criticises me
Anger if someone criticises me
Recoiling when my partner touches me
Anger if anyone cuddles me
Back pain
Extreme PMT
Blurry vision before I have to speak publicly
Migraines
My constant, unshifting anxiety
The sudden fear and overwhelm when I walk into a
    church
The sudden anger and shame when I see a happy family
Insomnia
Early menopause
The nausea I feel when I get my haircut
Screaming at my kids when they're too noisy
My stress – I'm always, always, always stressed
Getting floaty and spaced out at the weirdest times
How my hearing gets all weird and muffled if I'm
    stressed

Mind
Brutal negative thinking
Fear of being late
Chronic fear of being early
Fear of driving far away from home
Fear of driving at night

Forgetfulness
Confusion
Brain fog
Need to be liked
Need to be better than anyone else in the room
My constant need to prove myself
Hatred of God and religion
Hatred of men
Hatred of women
How much I hate myself
Daydreaming and fantasising
The decision not to join a sports team
Poor word recall
Poor short-term memory
Poor long-term memory
My temporary inability to speak

Behaviours
Binge eating
Under-eating
Anorexia
Constant yo-yo dieting
My relentless attempts to please everyone
My desperate attempts to keep a friend at any cost
The need to be punished using S&M
My abusive relationship pattern
How I end every relationship just as we're about
    to commit
Drug-taking

Alcohol use and misuse
Shopping addiction
How I can't hold down a job
Under-earning
My need to hoard money
The way I can't take care of myself
The plastic surgery I've had.

I'm going to stop, but I could go on and on. These aspects of people's lives are things they themselves attribute to their trauma. Seeing these physical issues, emotions, thoughts, beliefs, cognitive issues, neurological symptoms and behaviours as ongoing *reactions* to a traumatic experience is helpful for many people. Despite its length, every single reaction included on this list can be placed into one of the categories in the Trauma Loop: body, mind or behaviour. And every single one keeps us trapped within our reactions and within our trauma.

In this book I'm not going to explain the detailed neurological, emotional and behavioural mechanisms linking a traumatic experience to under-earning (although I'd have a good go at it!). Instead, I'm presenting you with an idea – that if you reframe your current issues in terms of your past trauma (reactions to a past threat), you may be able to join some dots.

The list above speaks to me. It takes trauma to a whole new level. It helps me better understand my trauma. I hope it helps you better understand yours. Everything on that list relates to the survival response and demonstrates how trauma pushes us to unusual places. Traumas can affect everything. The overwhelm, the sense of ongoing threat and fear, the powerlessness and the shame put their sticky, shitty little tendrils into every corner of our lives.

What is a traumatic reaction? It's anything you tell me it is.

Triggered

I've used the term *trigger* or *triggered* many times in the book so far. Although I included a little explanation in chapter one, we need to get clear about triggers here because understanding them is central to how you're going to break free from your past. Before I emigrated from the UK, a lot of my friends were in recovery. (Well, they still are, I'm just a million miles away.) Do you know what I mean when I say *recovery*? It means they're 12-step fellowship people. They're emotionally sober and proud. They've faced their compulsive, addictive behaviour and the damaging thinking that drives it. In inspiring and humbling ways, they've faced their trauma and their pain. The reason I mention them is because when you run with this recovery crowd in London, LA, Berlin, Sydney or wherever else, you're going to hear the word *triggered* a lot.

'I was so triggered at the weekend.'

'Oh, you have no idea, I was soooooo triggered at the weekend.'

'Hearing you say you were triggered makes me so triggered right now.'

'Oh, nightmare.'

'Total nightmare.'

I jest, but I want you to know that in some circles the term *triggered* is used often. People who are in one of the 12-step fellowships, who have done a load of therapy, or who watch *Dr Phil* on repeat *get it*. Maybe you use the word? If you do, I'm interested in when and how you use it. Because the word is inherently linked to trauma – it's a psychological term used to describe the process of being subconsciously reminded of a painful past experience.

A trigger can be anything – a smell, image, sound, word, internal bodily sensation, action, thought, person, situation – that reminds us of the past experience. These triggers activate the unprocessed memory, which then provokes the initial reaction, throwing us back into the survival response. For example, a trigger (e.g. being criticised) reminds us of a past traumatic experience (e.g. an insecure parental relationship). The trigger activates the unprocessed trauma memory and the fight, flight, freeze response. We are thrown back into our past and we embody aspects of who we were at the time of the initial experience. We lose the present and we lose our adult self. We – literally – repeat the past.

If this process wasn't so damaging I'd rave about it because, in biological terms, it's completely mind-blowing. Really, it's incredible. Say we experienced a threat at the age of ten years old. Because we were extremely overwhelmed the experience wasn't properly processed. If we're reminded of the initial experience even twenty years later, the original survival response returns. Is it maladaptive or protective?

I like to embrace my trigger-response and recognise that my body is trying to keep me safe. It wants me well. It wants me to recognise when there's a threat and it wants me to protect myself. My body loves me. It triggers to protect me. Recognising the loving role of triggers is critical. They're not a sign you're broken or unwell. They're not a sign your body hates you. They're your body's way of speaking to you. It's saying: *beware, keep safe.* It's also saying: *there's stuff here, old stuff, that I need you to face.* Triggers are hard, yes. But they're also your pathway to a new life. If we can embrace them, rather than push them away. If we draw them to us, stand in them, *feel* them, we can grow beyond our wildest dreams.

Recognising your own unique triggers is half the battle. Those recovery people I described are going to be just fine. Why? Because they *get* it. They know how it feels to be triggered so they can map their triggers and their trauma. They can find loving strategies to help them reconnect to their body, their adult self and their unbreakable core after they've been triggered. They can recognise and *own* their triggered state until they gradually return to the present moment and their adult self. By doing so, they don't make *their* trigger about someone or something that in reality has little to do with their extreme reaction.

Being triggered is uncomfortable. Oh, let's be real, it's much more than that. Being triggered can be intensely painful. It can shatter a moment, a day or a week. When we're triggered we're often thrown back into the same sense of fear, overwhelm or powerlessness we had at the time of the initial trauma. Because of this, the idea of success, abundance or meaningful change can seem impossible. Growth can seem so completely out of reach, because we're powerless . . . again. If we experience a strong triggered reaction, nothing seems possible. Our world and our hopes are obliterated. Our power evaporates. We disconnect from our instinct, our strength and our self. It's really . . . shit.

You know the worst possible thing you can do when you're triggered? Not realise you're triggered.

If we get that we're *in it*, *it* does less damage. *It* can be observed. If we can see that *it* is not about today or who we are today, we can regain our power. By calling it out (*I've been triggered, so I'm feeling ashamed*) we intervene in the overwhelm. We intervene in the powerlessness. We intervene in the traumatic thinking. We don't fall back on traumatic coping.

We step into our strong adult self to remind our younger self (the one we've been thrown back to) that all is okay. We intervene in the loop, with love.

Reactions vs action

I want to talk about the difference between reactions and actions. For example, perhaps as you begin to observe your triggers, you notice you're triggered into a shutdown reaction every time a man publicly undermines you. But if a woman does this to you, you respond from within yourself. You stay connected to your core. You feel angry and frustrated, and you tell her so. You feel adrenaline, but it's protective and it feels good. You put down a firm boundary that lets her know that you will not allow her to publicly undermine you. Whereas if a man does this, you feel completely powerless, you get spaced out, you can't concentrate, you want to cry, you're anxious, ashamed, you want to run away and hide forever. Your thinking spirals – *I'm such a failure, why do I always embarrass myself?*

These different responses to a similar event teach you something about your past trauma. The fact you experienced a traumatic reaction to the man but not the woman tells you something about your past traumatic experiences. It lets you know that, quite possibly, you experienced a traumatic reaction when a man publicly undermined you in your past. I know this clarity sounds too good to be true, but for many it is this clear: if we closely watch and observe our reactions we learn about our past traumas, and what we need to heal.

In this example, you had an uncontrollable *reaction* to the man. But when the woman crossed that same line, you took *action* instead. A reaction is uncontrolled. It leaps out of us. Reactions happen when we're triggered in some way. If these reactions are repetitive or extreme, they may relate to a past trauma. When we *act*, we are present. We are in our body, in the moment, in our current life and connected to our core and our adult. We may feel compelled to respond, but we have control. This is what we're shooting for. We need you to step into a life of action, not reaction.

If it's hysterical, it's historical.

Have you heard this recovery phrase before? It's a little corny, but in my experience it's a profoundly true statement.

The bigger someone's reaction, the more likely it is that it stems from a past hurt. When someone overreacts to something you've said, when they lose it, it's not about now. It's not about you. It's about a past moment or relationship that caused them deep pain, or a trauma that hasn't been healed. The same is true of you. When you overreact, something from your past has been triggered. Figuring out what you're overreacting to, when you're overreacting and how you're overreacting will help you spot the patterns you need to break. It will help you find your trauma.

Stress head?

I just want to say a little something about stress. Traumatic stress is a thing. In fact, it's the clinical name for trauma symptoms that don't meet the level required to be diagnosed with PTSD. I'm going to keep this brief, and I mention it for one reason and one reason alone. People who live with unresolved traumatic reactions are often stress heads. It doesn't take much for their alarm system to activate. They react instead of act. Their window of tolerance for life stressors tends to be (but is not always) lower than those without trauma. The smallest to-do can trigger a huge response because emotion regulation is difficult. Living in this constant stressed-out, frazzled state is exhausting.

I've mentioned this because, even though 'easily stressed' is there, clear as day, in the Appendix, it's often overlooked or minimised. Nowadays, people are *supposed* to be stressed, right? Supposed to be manic and busy? Unfortunately, yes, in many modern cultures there's an expectation that we're all a little strung out. This expectation means that those living with traumatic stress don't recognise that it is what it is – an ongoing reaction to a perceived threat from a long time ago. So, if you're perpetually stressed, frazzled, feeling unable to cope, overwhelmed, stretched, strung out, spread too thin, or whatever other word or phrase you tend to use, be aware that it can be a symptom.

High stress and overwhelm are not good for our body or our mind. It's also not good for those around us, or for our relationships with those around us. As we heal and reconnect to our body, our unbreakable core and our adult self, we will gently find ways to better control all those arousal hormones, remain present and rebalance.

Post-traumatic stress disorder (PTSD)

In the section above on triggers, I make being triggered sound manageable and growth-inducing. This certainly isn't the case for people with extremely high levels of trauma symptoms, or people who have just experienced a severe trauma. For these people, triggers are often overwhelming and frightening. Triggers can take them to dark places, and returning to one's self can feel like a battle, not like returning home to a safe place.

Post-traumatic stress disorder (PTSD) is the name given to the prolonged experience of multiple, more extreme, trauma symptoms. Complex PTSD (C-PTSD) is the name given to the prolonged experience of trauma symptoms resulting from ongoing, severe traumas (for example, child abuse or domestic violence).[4] People who've experienced these kinds of severe, long-term traumas are likely to experience many of the PTSD symptoms, but will also be more prone to finding relationships difficult, cutting themselves off from people, dissociation and shame, among other things.[5] Living with PTSD or C-PTSD can be very hard, and recovering from it can require years of self-love, therapy, support and commitment. When high levels of symptoms are present, the body often doesn't feel like a safe place to retreat. Instead, at times it can feel like your body is trying to harm you. Your body is on fire with hypervigilance and it's triggered to the extreme. When trauma symptoms are very high, the goal isn't abundance and growth, it's getting through the day. It's taking small steps to heal the body and the spirit. PTSD or C-PTSD can be exhausting and frightening. As I said in the introduction, if you have extremely elevated trauma symptoms, this book is unlikely to fully meet your needs at the moment. Use this book for information, but don't rely only on this as a self-help tool – find meaningful, one-to-one support.

I never took a clinical measure for PTSD. Throughout my therapy sessions we talked in terms of trauma and grief, pain and loss, not disorders. In fact, I remember this moment with my therapist:

Me: Shit, do you think I've got PTSD.
My therapist, with a caring smile on her face: Let's just say, I don't think it's a coincidence that you chose to dedicate your life to understanding PTSD.

Me (awestruck): Is it super weird that this is the first time I've realised this?

My therapist: We're all drawn to things that heal us.

Me (thinking): Oh, you are so wise you should be the Queen.

If I'd completed a clinical diagnostic measure of PTSD at various stages in my life, I'd have been found to have extremely elevated trauma symptoms. PTSD. I didn't complete this measure because I worked with therapists who talked in terms of trauma, not PTSD. Clinical psychologists tend to diagnose; psychotherapists tend not to. Neither approach is better or worse: there's joy in their differences, and variety within trauma treatment is greatly needed.

In this book, and in all my work, I talk in terms of trauma, grief, pain and loss, instead of diagnoses and disorders. I talk about your unique reactions to awful, terrifying experiences. I do not at any point tell you there is anything *wrong* with you, because there isn't. I won't buy into the fact that you're broken. I'm going to need you to get on board with this idea. If you want to change anything, you're going to have to step into warrior mode. It's about taking personal responsibility for your future. It's about owning your power – hard when you've spent a lifetime being triggered into powerlessness. Hard, but time.

Part 2

How trauma affects your life

Chapter Four

How trauma affects your relationships

This chapter might feel heavy at times. Relationships are hard. A major source of this hard, heavy, confusing, painful feeling is trauma. This feeling is not clear-cut. It can feel like we're trying to walk through mud; it's a muddy pain. Or, put more simply, it's the effect of our unresolved past *stuff* on our present day. We're all trying to forge ahead and create great lives. We're trying to build beautiful, meaningful relationships with our partners, family and friends. But often the relationships go wrong. We find ourselves repeating arguments, destructive behaviours, patterns and dynamics.

I do, of course, meet some people who feel completely fulfilled by their relationships. But more often, I meet people who are overwhelmed and confused about why the people they love are the source of so much of their pain. They sit in the muddy pain, repeating and repeating, trying and trying.

I think, and hope, that if we all tool up on trauma and begin to view our current relationship behaviour as a response to past hurt, we will be able to shift this muddy pain and start having more joyful, spontaneous relationships.

Provided that it isn't born from abuse, bullying, neglect or extreme dysfunction, most muddy pain is *normal*. It's not a sign that we're messed up or fundamentally damaged, but that we're human. We all have a past. We were all raised a certain way – some in very functional, healthy, happy homes, many others in dysfunctional, unhealthy or destructive homes. Many are left carrying relational or attachment trauma. On top of that, at least 70 per cent of us have experienced a big-T trauma,[1] and many more again have experienced other-t traumas. These traumas often leave us with a sense of powerlessness or helplessness. They leave us with a sense of fear, anger or shame. We *react* to life from within our trauma instead of *acting* from a place of grounded, adult core-connection. The good news is, you have a choice. You can repeat and repeat, or you can break the loop and step forward into new relationship patterns.

Be relationship brave

There are many ways I could dive into this conversation about trauma and relationships, but I'm going to start by telling you that although the muddy pain isn't abnormal, our response to it often is. We respond in a way that perpetuates the pain, but we don't have to. We can step out of the cycle. As we do, we realise that our muddy pain is both the source of discomfort and our path to freedom.

About six months ago my friend Meg called me. She'd spent all weekend at her new partner's apartment in the city. They'd been together for about three months and it was starting to get serious (ooh la la). She was happy, and I was happy too, because her previous partners had been – how can I say this politely – jerks. They'd been mean or drunk, or mean *and* drunk. She hadn't dated anyone for over a year before she met Chris, her new partner. During that time she'd been living on her own and had been in therapy most of the year. She started a new job and was doing more yoga than I thought humanly possible. She was, you know, doing it. Over the year I saw her transform – not into perfection, but into herself. She'd decided enough was enough. She was totally over romantic relationships, and recognised the dysfunction they had always led to. She wanted more and intuitively knew that was only possible if she dealt with her stuff, looked at her past and reconnected to herself. And then Chris came along.

Given that Meg had spent all weekend at Chris's place, I was waiting for a raunchy exposé of the weekend, but instead she told me something I wasn't expecting. Something that I think you need to hear, because it will help you see what's possible in relationships. And yes, this example is from a romantic relationship, but it could just as easily apply to a friendship or a family relationship.

Chris and Meg hadn't been getting on. They'd been bickering and had some blow-out fights. They were both more disappointed about this than in previous relationships, because each had thought it would *be* different because it *felt* different. Chris suggested that Meg should come over so they could talk, and both of them sensed that it could be a bad, let's-call-it-quits kind of conversation. When Meg arrived on the Friday night and Chris opened the door, they held each other tightly and then, without really knowing why, they both started crying. Meg said they stood in the hallway for what felt like half an hour, and when they pulled away, Chris told her how sad he'd been feeling, and how confused he was about what was going on.

They sat down on the lounge and started talking. Meg said they talked all night, about everything that mattered. They talked about how Chris was raised, and how his mother and father were pretty absent from his life. He told her about his father's drinking and the time he was sent to live with his aunt in Florida. He hesitantly told her that some awful things had happened to him while he was living at his aunt's house. As they continued to talk, Chris revealed how alone he had felt all his life, and that he desperately wanted a healthy loving relationship. How he felt that Meg had this incredible life separate to his and although her success and independence was amazing to him, deep down it also made him worry she would leave. How he'd been too afraid to go to therapy, and that he admired her so much for jumping in. He told her he loved her, and he wanted to do what it took to make it work.

Meg was crying as she told me this. She was overwhelmed, not with grief but with relief and hope. What she saw, when Chris opened up, was a man who was capable of great love and who wanted a deep commitment. He wanted her in his life, but for a man who hadn't been shown how to love and carried huge fear and sadness stemming from his own past pain, it was also overwhelming and confusion-inducing. His past – his trauma – made things muddy and painful. He was still reacting, but he desperately wanted to stop.

Then Meg told Chris about her past relationships. She told him that her biggest fear was that they would go the same way – that he'd end up mean and drunk and she'd end up angry, afraid and alone. She told Chris about how abusive and violent many of these past relationships were, one in particular. She told Chris about how upset she got when Chris drank more than two beers, or how frightened she felt when she smelled beer on his breath as he kissed her.

She told him about the death of her mum when she was seventeen years old. How her life, from losing her mum until this year – which had brought therapy, yoga, a new job and Chris – had been a dysfunctional, awful mess. She told him she had sensed that Chris was afraid of her independence, and this made her confused and angry. She said she tried so hard, every day, to be the person she wanted to be – to make healthy, mature choices – but it wasn't easy. She told him that what she wanted to do, really, was give up, but instead she continued going to yoga and meeting her friends for coffee because she made a commitment to herself. She said she was trying so hard and she needed his support. Because if she went back to how it was, it would be terrible for both of them.

These two wonderful, brave people had the conversation we all need to have, when we're ready, with the people we love deeply. They talked about, and owned, their feelings and their trauma. They talked about how their past was affecting their relationship today, and what they needed to do to break free. Remember what I said at the beginning of the chapter?

. . . we realise that our muddy pain is both the source of discomfort and our path to freedom.

Chris and Meg stood in their pain. They were honest about their past, owning their feelings and behaviour. The muddy pain of their relationship is the source of their unnerving discomfort. It reminds them of their past and their deepest hurts. The muddy pain brings stuff up. But because they were able to own it, see it and voice it, they used it as a way of growing beyond their past. As they follow this process (as painful as it can be), they will grow; they will overcome; they will develop the type of relationship that they are both longing for.

Be relationship brave. If you are, you'll develop deep mutual understanding and you'll heal some of that old *stuff*. In platonic relationships this approach is optional, although highly recommended within your closest, deepest friendships. In committed romantic relationships it's not optional: it's a necessity. If you and your partner can be open about your past pain; if you can openly discuss what triggers you; if you can share your negative thinking; if you can recognise the coping mechanisms that you fall back on . . . if you can do this, all the past *stuff*, all the trauma, is surmountable.

Notes on brave conversations

1. You do not need to discuss the details of your traumatic experiences. This is unnecessary and can be re-traumatising. I have been married for ten years. My partner and I have talked about our traumas, but not once have we discussed the experiences in detail. To do so could cause us harm. The same goes for my friendships: I know about my friends' pasts without knowing everything; just as they know about my past without knowing everything. When we're ready, we let the people we love know that we're still reacting to experiences from our past. We do this so we can put down the shame, break the loop and move on. Please remember: to heal, we don't need to retell, rehash or 'go there' at all. It is enough to say that *something happened*.
2. You don't need to have these conversations today. Honesty and openness within healthy, loving friendships and relationships is something we work towards, not something we have to challenge ourselves with unnecessarily. We work on ourselves first, always.

Uncomfortable is okay

Committed relationships, whether they're romantic or platonic, take courage at times. All relationships, even the great ones, can be painful. For most of us, walking out feels easier at one point or another. I've been so close to bailing on my marriage (I mean, not actually, but I've *felt* right there). Then, usually, this happens: I call my dearest friend. She listens, I listen, and at some point I say:

'Okay, I get it, just another opportunity for some more oh-so-painful personal growth.'

Don't get me wrong, I fully support leaving a relationship at the right moment, when all the learning and growth is done. But many people bail before then because they're afraid of what they're confronted with. When it feels uncomfortable, painful or overwhelming, there's a strong impulse to avoid it all. We often can't (or won't) discuss these painful feelings. Here, I'm not talking about the type of big, brave conversation Meg and Chris had. I'm talking about everyday honesty. I'm talking about telling our friends, family and partners how we feel. Being able to look someone in the eyes and tell them our fears. Being able to tell someone if they've hurt us and say sorry if we've hurt them. Being able to say, 'Yes, let's meet for coffee and talk', even though you know it'll be awkward and uncomfortable. I'm talking about truth and vulnerability. I'm talking about not running away, even though every fibre of your being wants to book a one-way flight to Costa Rica.

If we grew up in a house that welcomed all of our feelings (the easy, positive ones and the tricky, challenging ones), we're likely to be less intimidated by relationships today because we can feel, voice and own our feelings without fear and shame.

If we grew up in a house where all parts of our ourselves (even the behaviours that didn't serve us) were accepted, today we're likely to be less intimidated by relationships because we know that our behaviour doesn't affect our worth or lovableness. This means we're more likely to own our mistakes without fear and shame.

If we grew up in a house where all of our thoughts, beliefs and questions (including the ones that challenged our parents) were met with interest, today we're less likely to be intimidated by relationships because we know that our thoughts are not facts. They can be voiced without fear and shame.

Most people do not grow up in this kind of house, so relationships can feel intimidating and hard. The pain of some of our past interactions can make interactions today feel confusing and overwhelming. I'm not just talking about romantic relationships, I'm talking about all relationships. Socialising, acquaintances, friendships, work relationships – they can all feel really overwhelming at times. It's okay if you don't fully get relationships. It really is okay. Let yourself learn – I had to. We don't have to rush in, we can take our time.

Why bother with all this discomfort? Why not avoid it, stick our fingers in our ears and find someone who (at least temporarily) makes us feel more comfortable? Because respectful adult relationships can help us heal the damaging messages and traumatic beliefs we developed when we were younger. Standing in front of people you trust, allowing yourself to voice your true feelings and thoughts and show your true self will help you heal. To be truly seen and heard by another helps heal the old relationship wounds of the past – a past in which many of us were not fully seen and heard.

Relationships can be hard. Marriage and families can be hard; raising kids can be hard. Friendships can be hard. Other people can be hard work. And yet, what's the point of life without meaningful connection? Growth is painful because we have to face the stuff that's blocking us from fully accessing these connections. Relationships are hard, yes. But we can only fully heal ourselves in relation to others when we are taking part in healthy, respectful, flexible adult relationships.

What I'm not saying

The problem with writing a book, sending a tweet, or posting on Facebook is that I have very little control over what other people make my words mean. We all – myself included – take something someone has said and apply our own meaning and context to it. We project our own stuff onto other people. We're humans; that's just what we do. Even people who've done a tonne of work on themselves do it – it's impossible not to. So, in this chapter, as I talk about courage in relationships, I want to be very clear about what I'm saying . . . and what I'm *not* saying.

I am saying . . . to fully heal ourselves in relation to others and to heal relational trauma, we have to be *in* relationships. Depending on our past, we might begin by focusing on a relationship with a psychotherapist or a counsellor. Yes, this counts. A therapeutic relationship can be, and often is, the first relationship we heal within. All I'm saying is that there have to be other people involved. They can be counsellors, work colleagues, friends in a support group, a club you're part of, your acquaintances from the gym, old friends, new friends, family members, your partner, whoever. As long as the relationship is respectful and has potential for growth, it can help us learn and grow. These relationships won't be perfect and pain-free because perfect and pain-free only exist in Disney movies. And thank God they aren't perfect, because perfect doesn't help us grow. You'll learn about relationships because of the imperfections; because of the awkwardness; because of the uncomfortable moments. Because of the vulnerability.

I am not saying we have to be in a romantic relationship to heal. I am not saying that *any* relationship is a good relationship and that you should commit to *any* relationship because any relationship is better than being alone. I am not saying that someone can treat you badly and you should put up with it because you're trying to heal yourself in relation to others. I am not saying that you should prioritise a relationship over your wellbeing. I am not saying that boundaries don't matter. I am not saying that healing only takes places in relationships. I am not saying that you should focus on relationships with others before you focus on your relationship with yourself.

Relational trauma and all relationship issues can only be fully healed when we are taking part in relationships. But we should focus on ourselves first and foremost. And when we are ready to look at our relationships, the ones we take part in have to be good enough. There has to be respect. Abusive relationships, relationships with narcissists who take no responsibility, emotionally manipulative relationships, violent relationships, destructive relationships, toxic friendships – these are all examples of destructive, crazy-making relationships (which are traumatic in and of themselves). These relationships can't be navigated. These are the ones we have to leave, because the damage outweighs the potential for growth. If certain lines are crossed, healing and growth is an impossibility, so get out.

What I am saying is that relationships take courage, but there's a difference between courage and self-annihilation. Uncomfortable at times is okay; abusive is not. If you're unsure where the line is, get in touch with someone: speak to your therapist or to a trusted friend. Figure out if the relationship is a potential source of growth if you stay, or if your growth will come as you leave.

Real relationships

The above sections demonstrate some of what we all *should* be doing in relationships. The evil *shoulds*. They've caused me no end of hell in my own life, so let's not apply the same pressure to you as you lift yourself up and out of old relationship patterns. In among all the *shoulds*, the most useful sentence I wrote in the past few pages is this:

Relationships are hard.

Yes. They are. And trauma makes them harder. Before I dive into *how* trauma affects relationships, I want to give you some real-life examples. These are quotes from real people who have generously agreed to share their stories with me. Some of these people carry severe big-T trauma; some carry other-t trauma; some carry attachment trauma from relationships with their parents; some carry relational trauma. Some *know* they carry trauma, and for others it's buried trauma. They are *normal* people getting on with *normal* life.

'Sometimes, when I've had a really hard day, say something really shitty happened at work, I just can't handle the kids in the evening. I end up shouting at them, screaming at them, and I know I shame them. It all just pours out, all this hate and upset. I actually can't believe I do it.'

'This might sound weird, but when I'm with my parents I just kind of shut down. One minute, as I walk to the restaurant to meet them, I'm pumped about work and life, and then after I've been with them for a few minutes I just go flat. It's like I retreat. I get all small and weird. I try and take part in the conversation, but it's sort of like I'm watching it happen.'

'I feel like I mess up a lot of close friendships because I always have to prove myself. I show off, I gloat and I brag. After I've done it I know I have, and commit to not doing it again, but it always happens. There's this switch and I just go into alpha-male hyper drive.'

'People say I'm confident and I think I can be, but I also find socialising really hard. I get so anxious and feel incredibly bad about myself when I'm in a group of people. Usually it's after I've been silly or brash, and I feel like I've crossed the line. I feel so upset with myself because I've told a ridiculous joke or said something in a certain tone of voice, and I just get this sense that I've upset someone or that someone doesn't like me. I spend the rest of the night so anxious, and trying to make it up to the other person in weird indirect ways.'

'My partner can get so grumpy and just stonewall me for days. He had a really difficult, often abusive, relationship with his mum, so I do get it. But I feel so sad when he's like that. I'm just in this awful anxious bubble, watching my phone, until he comes around. He doesn't apologise, but in his own way he lets me know he's moved on. As soon as he does, my anxiety goes away and we're okay again.'

'If my partner says she doesn't want to be intimate I totally shut down. It's worse when I'm already having a bad day. If something happened and I'm already feeling bad, and then she turns me down, that's it – shame, depression, whatever. It's all just too much.'

'I've only had one long-term relationship – it lasted about two years. The others have been a few months.

I get that the common denominator is me, so I'm probably the issue, but I find men impossible. The guys I've dated were aggressive, rude and volatile. They were so teenage when I criticised them. It's just the same thing, over and over again. I become the same person too – they say something and I say something, and they say something, and I'm back in this familiar bad situation. My friends keep telling me to date a different type of guy, but it makes no difference – it always ends up the same.'

'I feel like, if I'm honest, most of my messages to my close friends should read: "Why haven't you messaged me back? What did I do wrong? I know I'm a terrible human being, please let me prove my love to you!" I don't think my friends know I'm like this if they don't get in touch. I'm trying to make it sound all light and like I can control my reaction, but I can't. Sometimes it really hurts. I just feel alone and not good enough.'

'Am I allowed to talk about sex?! This is a big issue for us. If my partner suddenly touches me, like out of the blue or I'm not expecting it, I want to punch him. This rage rises up in me. I just feel so angry. Sometimes I have this feeling as we have sex. Pure rage. I feel so sad saying this, because I don't want to be this person and my partner doesn't deserve it.'

'Sometimes when my girlfriend touches me I feel really ashamed. It's really intense. I was raised in a religious home, so maybe it links to that, but I've also had some intimate experiences I'm really ashamed of. So maybe it's more to do with that. I don't really know. I feel upset admitting it's an issue for me.'

'Last week my girlfriend and I had a fight about money. She doesn't earn that much at the moment, which she hates, and she goes insane if I mention it. We were talking about holidays and all I said was, "It'll be great when you're promoted next year so we have a bigger holiday budget," and she just blew up. Like totally lost it. Anyway, she's screaming at me about how I don't value her, and I've just totally had enough and I want to walk out. I open a bottle of wine and pour myself a bucketful and she does the same, and it just turns into this full-on raging argument. She actually threw something at me.'

Pure, unadulterated honesty. Thank you.

We could get very complicated as we try to explain each of these unique, painful situations. Oh my word, people make up all sorts of stuff about what is going on in these moments. People talk and talk and blame and shame. Here's what I think is happening for every person:

They were triggered.

The people in these stories have been reminded of something from their past. For some it's being touched; for others it's being spoken to aggressively. For one it's seeing their parents; for another it's hearing that they don't earn enough money. For one it's a complicated web of triggers that leads to the repetition of destructive relationships; for another it's feeling rejected. They're triggered by something outside of the relationship or something within the relationship. The effects of being triggered are deeply harmful. They're all thrown back into *old* reactions. Some run, some fight, some try to control, some zone out and some shut down. Whatever the response, it stems from the past and it keeps them locked in the past. Remember the Trauma Loop? That's what we see in these quotes. Their sense of threat, over-whelm or powerlessness is triggered, and it pushes them to their own unique cascade of reactions, feelings, thoughts and coping mechanisms. The Trauma Loop is the source of the *muddy pain* I've been talking about: repetitive, extreme, confusing reactions that disconnect us from who we really are and what our heart desires for our relationships.

Triggers

All triggers will affect us and our relationships, but what I'm trying to do in this section is help you pinpoint your *relationship* triggers. These are things that happen within our relationships today that remind us of a past trauma and set off our traumatic reaction. We'll cover reactions in the next section – for now we're just thinking about triggers. Common relationship triggers are listed below. Ugh. A list, I know. But within this murky, complicated, relational topic, we need to find clarity. And I don't know about you, but lists always help me get clearer.

- Conflict and disagreement
- Someone being stressed/anxious/angry/overwhelmed around us
- Feeling unseen, unheard or misunderstood (someone not saying hi, ignoring you or not trying to understand your point of view)
- Feeling like your needs aren't met (someone making a choice on your behalf or not considering what you want/need)
- Being disrespected or *feeling* disrespected (someone mocking you publicly, or speaking to you rudely)
- Being criticised or *feeling* criticised
- Perceiving the other person as emotionally withdrawing or being unavailable (someone ignoring your calls or messages, someone not giving you eye contact or shutting down)
- Feeling abandoned (someone walking away from a conversation, being given the silent treatment, someone ignoring your calls or messages)
- Feeling unloved (someone not smiling at you, someone avoiding you or speaking to you in a harsh tone of voice)
- Feeling disliked (not being invited somewhere, or being laughed at)
- Boundary crossing (not being listened to when you say no, invading your personal space, someone taking on your responsibilities without you asking them to)

- Feeling rejected (someone not cuddling you back, not wanting physical touch)
- Sex, touch, cuddling
- Feeling stressed/overwhelmed/out of control (your own internal physiological triggers)
- Feeling threatened or attacked
- Healthy independence (someone takes a few days to reply to a message, your partner goes away for the weekend)
- Healthy dependence (someone needing you or relying on you).

Your relationship triggers are the parts of your relationships today that somehow remind you of your past traumatic experiences. The reminders are often subconscious and subtle, but the reaction can be very strong. We can get triggered in all types of relationships. This is about friendships and family gatherings. It's about your relationship with your kids, work relationships, marriage and casual one-night stands. It's about your big relationships and your little ones.

What you'll find, though, is that your triggers reflect your own unique past pain, grief, loss and trauma. So although these triggers can occur in all relationships, you might find that your best friend not answering her phone doesn't *mean* anything to you (it holds no charge), but your partner not answering his phone somehow reminds you of a past trauma, so provokes a traumatic reaction. A trigger in one type of relationship or with a certain type of person can be inconsequential in the context of another relationship.

I know I've made this point before, but it's critical. We are in the subjective, undefined world of trauma. What you're doing is trying to join the dots so you can break free. You're spotting patterns in your own physical sensations, emotions, cognitions and behaviours.

Before we go into more detail about the myriad of reactions that can occur once you've been triggered in a relationship, I highly recommend that you take a break. We've covered a lot of information, so go on, put the kettle on.

Reactions

You read about traumatic reactions in the previous chapter, so you know that the relationship triggers I've just outlined can take you *anywhere*. Although this is true, the above relational triggers commonly lead on to some specific relational reactions. Some of these – shame, for example – you've seen before, but others are specific to relationships. They're all part of the Trauma Loop: physical, emotional, mental and/or behavioural reactions to reminders of our past pain. Before you look at the relationship reactions, I want to be very clear about the process. The trigger (see pp. 109 to 111) is the reminder, the reaction is the trauma. For example:

Sex (the trigger) may lead to dissociation (the reaction).

Someone rejecting you (the trigger) can lead to a painful shame spiral (the reaction).

Conflict (the trigger) can set off our subconscious *victim belief* and accompanying behaviours (the reaction).

Now that you're clear on the process, here are some common relationship reactions:

- Overwhelm (*these feelings are too much, this relationship is too much, life is too much*)
- Insecurity, anxiety and worry about the relationship, and then everything (*she's going to leave me, he doesn't love me, my life is a mess, everything is going wrong*)
- Uncontrolled aggression and rage at the other person, and then everything (*I hate her, I wish I'd never met him, I wish she would die, I hate my life . . . but mainly I hate them*)
- Blame, shame or both (*I think you're an arsehole and to blame for everything . . . I'm to blame for everything and I'm a terrible person . . . oh the shame, the crippling shame*)
- Self-righteousness (*how dare you; do you not realise I AM RIGHT*)
- Perfectionism (*I'm so afraid you'll leave I'm going to act as if I'm perfect until you do*)
- False arrogance (*I'm the best, I'm the best, I'm the best . . . I think*)
- Victim (*poor me, please someone fix me*)
- Persecutor (*I'm going to aggressively highlight everything you've ever done wrong . . . so I don't ever have to consider my part in this*)
- Fix-it (*can't bear the uncomfortable feelings, so let's make a plan . . . or ten*)

- People-pleasing (*can I get you some soup or make your bed . . . PLEASE LOVE ME*)
- People-provocation (*I'm going to wind you up until you prove me right and leave me*)
- Anger-driven, grumpy avoidance (*I'm going to stomp around the house, avoid eye contact and then huff off to bed*)
- Anxiety-driven, worried avoidance (*I'm going to nervously tidy the house while worrying . . . then watch something melancholic on Netflix*)
- Confusion and/or brain fog (*I know you want a conversation, but I'm at about 10 per cent brain function right now*)
- Disconnects or dissociates (*I'm checking out of here, off to Trauma Town on a hazy journey of self-hatred. . . bye relationship, bye self, bye body*)
- Traumatic thinking (*I'm a piece of shit . . . you're a piece of shit . . . we're both pieces of shit*)
- Traumatic coping (*I'm pressing the self-destruct button and having a drink, cigarette, food, binge . . . insert your own dysfunctional coping mechanism here*)

These are common traumatic reactions to the relationship triggers I listed earlier in the chapter. You're triggered and inside you're all fight, flight, freeze, but outside you're all passive-aggressive behaviour, confusion, people-pleasing, Netflix, wine, whatever. A trigger, then the reactions which dump that muddy pain all over you and your relationship.

This isn't really an exercise kind of book

Although this isn't really an exercise kind of book, I really would encourage you to take a moment (and maybe a piece of paper!) to consider which of your relationships are really triggering for you. Relationships can be confusing and over-whelming for everyone, but this is particularly true if you carry trauma. Because relationships are confusing, it helps if we take a moment to find some clarity when we need to. So if you're feeling wobbly, confused or overwhelmed because of what you've read, just take a beat. Grab a piece of paper and try to unpick things. That's the whole point of this book – helping you join the dots between your past and your today, so you can *break the loop*. Because clarity and awareness always bring about change and growth.

First, have a think about which of your relationships feel difficult and uncomfortable at the moment. Choose one to focus on. Next, take a moment to slow down your breathing before you step into thinking about this tricky relationship. If you need to, refer back to the grounding techniques on pages 41 and 42 to help you connect to yourself today. As you move through this exercise, return to the breath (slow deep breaths into your belly – in for the count of four, out for the count of eight, focusing on your belly) if you need. If it feels too much, stop completely. If this does happen, it's okay, you've learnt something invaluable: the relationship you're thinking about is highly triggering for you. Great information to discuss, with someone you trust, when you're ready.

 I had originally created a very structured exercise for you, but I think you're more likely to find your way with this if you free-write. Think about a time with the person you've chosen to focus on – a time that felt difficult or uncomfortable. As you write, think about these questions: Why was it difficult or uncomfortable? What happened? How did they behave? What did they say? How did you feel? How did you behave? Now, specifically try to hone in on your triggers and reactions. What triggered you? And how did you react?

There's no 'right' way to do this. Use full sentences, or one-word answers. Fill a whole journal with your thoughts and feelings, create a spider diagram, use highlighters. You can keep the page, or if you need to, you can tear it up and throw it in the bin. If it feels really shame-y and painful, burn it (safely please!). Do whatever you need.

Given that you've highlighted some trigger-points in your relationships, I want to tell you what I do, personally, when I'm triggered in my relationships. First, I acknowledge that I'm triggered, then I accept my reaction. Then I do what I can to return to a sense of safety and reconnect to my core. You can use these techniques too, if you need to.

1. **Acknowledge the reaction.** *I'm triggered because they hung up the phone, and I'm feeling overwhelmed and ashamed.* I then notice the uncomfortable feelings and sensations in my body, without trying to change them. Just notice and allow.

2. **Feel safer.** I do deep, slow polyvagal breathing (*e.g.* in for four, out for eight) to stimulate the vagus nerve and focus on affirmations (*I'm safe, I'm good enough, their reaction can't harm me, their reaction wasn't about me*). See the grounding techniques on pages 41 and 42 for other options.

3. **Connect to core.** I visualise a ball of light in my heart centre, breathe gently into it and affirm the connection to self (I connect to my core, my strength and my adult self).

4. **Discharge arousal energy.** If, as time goes on, I am anxious, elevated and on high alert, I notice the kinds of movements my body wants to make and I try to release some of the arousal energy (e.g. dance, punch the air, do a certain yoga pose or stretch). Then I repeat steps 1, 2 and 3.

Okay. You made it. We've done the relationship stuff. It gets easier from here on, I promise.

Chapter Five

How trauma affects your health

Unlike the previous murky, complicated relationship chapter, this chapter's pretty simple. We're going to look at two ways trauma affects your health. First, we're going to discuss dysfunctional coping and behaviours, then we're going to cover the long-term effects of trauma on the body.

Food, glorious food – or not

For many people, food and weight is a tricky subject. People who live in western countries where food is abundant tend to fall into one of two categories of eater. Put simply, people tend to either over- or under-eat. Often, how we eat relates to how we handle stress and negative feelings. So, as part of our conversation about how trauma affects your health, we need to consider how our feelings might affect the way we eat. The first category, over-eaters, eat more in response to their feelings. They eat when they're stressed, they eat for comfort. Most of them wish they didn't, but they do it because it's totally ingrained in them to reach for food (as a form of comfort) if they're upset, stressed, or in pain. The second group is people who eat less in response to stress. Unless they're extreme (e.g. anorexic) they're actually pretty happy they're built this way. In modern society, *skinny* is put on a pedestal, so their coping mechanism doesn't seem like a problem. For this second group it's about denying themselves comfort. It's about perfectionism and control, or rather the illusion of control. In an unpredictable world, exerting control, consciously or unconsciously, over our diet and body when we're stressed, makes some (albeit dysfunctional) sense.

Interestingly, all feelings, both negative and positive, can be projected onto the body and experienced through the process of eating. So excitement, for example, could be felt as an urge to either over-eat or under-eat. In their excitement, the over-eater might decide to go for a slap-up meal, whereas the under-eater may decide they're not hungry and grab a coffee instead. The transfer of feelings into food-behaviour is quick and often subconscious. They're habitual mechanisms that keep people trapped in certain behavioural patterns. It probably sounds fairly benign, but in its extreme it's very damaging. And aside from the toll on the body, this means people aren't able to experience the full glory of excitement. Instead, the happy sensations are immediately transferred *away*.

A person's eating behaviour can exist on a pendulum, where you swing from over- to under-eating, binge to diet, overconsumption to restriction, comfort to control. There's a normalcy to the pendulum when the swing is minor. Moving gradually from a healthy, more controlled diet to periods of relaxing, enjoying and indulging is common and unremarkable. This usually signals a healthy eater. This person is fluid and responsive with their diet, and they're not particularly aware of what their food or weight is doing on any given day. They may still lean towards either over-eating or under-eating in response to stress, but the mechanism is insignificant in terms of understanding them or their issues. They are not emotional eaters – their feelings tend to remain separate from their food.

But what about when the pendulum swing is bigger? What if someone's eating lurches from painful over-eating and binges tinged with a sense of failure and disgust to tightly controlled, white-knuckled dieting? This person's eating style is not insignificant. This person has a complicated relationship with food, and most likely, with their body, too. There are a lot of names for this type of eating. To make it sound fun a lot of people call it yo-yo dieting. But, of course, if you're one of these people, you know it's not fun at all. Food, eating and the body are often sources of great discomfort.

As well as the yo-yo dieters, there are the dysfunctional-but-committed types. For these people there's no lurching pendulum. They subconsciously committed to one of these self-destructive extremes many years ago and are still honouring that commitment today. They either predominantly over-eat, or predominantly under-eat. The over-eaters may sometimes try to clean up their eating, but it's done with little commitment or drive. The under-eaters may have some cake at Christmas or on their birthday, but essentially they always eat too little, and/or adhere to tight rules around their eating. There are a lot of reasons a person may have adopted an extreme form of eating. Nature is involved. Some are genetically predisposed to obesity and high food consumption, others are predisposed to slender frames and low food consumption. Nurture is involved. Some have been raised in homes where portions are large and big appetites are applauded, others are raised in homes where portions are restricted and small appetites are applauded. It's not all related to how we feel, but how we feel is highly relevant.

I've chosen to go into detail about food because we all eat and we all feel, so it's easy for the two to become entwined as we try to cope with life. Emotional eating, eating disorders, restrictive eating, binging, over-eating, purging, strict diets, junk food fetishes – these are just some of the many ways humans try to cope with their feelings through their food intake. Food should be a source of pleasure, health and nourishment, so it's an easy way of self-punishing if we're prone to hating on ourselves.

The crutch

All humans feel pain, loss, grief and trauma. All humans cope with this through one crutch or another. Some crutches are healthy and empowering, such as cycling or giving the garden a good prune. Other crutches are socially acceptable, but still destructive, like smoking or maxing out your credit card. Then there are the heavy-duty crutches, the ones that are all about self-destruction. Not all of these heavy-duty crutches involve abusing a substance (such as alcohol, narcotics, prescription drugs, sugar). People have found loads of destructive ways to cope that involve a process rather than a substance (such as shopping, over-exercising, over- or under-eating, sex, gaming, gambling, pornography). Whether there's a substance involved or not, all dysfunctional coping affects your health. It traps you in emotional, cognitive and behavioural loops, separates you from your feelings and your body, and takes you away from the present moment. Critically, these ways of coping – that are all about avoidance – prevent us from learning, growing and maturing in the way we need and deserve.

Addiction is a psychological and physical inability to stop taking a substance or engaging in an activity, even though it's causing you harm.[1] Not all crutches are addic-tions, but many can end up there. Whether your crutch is good for your body (such as gentle exercise when you're stressed) or less good for your body (such as drinking beer when you're stressed), either can become part of an addic-tive cycle. As we think about our own trauma loops, we need to figure out whether our coping is dysfunctional and causing us harm. We also need to establish if our coping is part of our traumatic reaction (i.e. a reaction to a trigger). Healthy coping is controlled and empowered. It's not part of our traumatic reaction. Traumatic coping is reactive, uncontrolled and disempowering. The coping itself is part of our traumatic reaction.

This chapter is my chapter. I'm all over it. Why? As an ex-anorexic, I obviously have a lot of things to say on the subjects of traumatic coping and addiction. (Quick pause, am I an 'ex-anorexic' or 'anorexic'? Alcoholics in 12-step programs still call themselves alcoholics even after they've stopped drinking, but I don't identify at all with being an anorexic anymore, so I'm going to do myself a solid and back what I just said – I'm an *ex*-anorexic.)

My crutch of choice – anorexia – is the go-to choice of people who want to fit in *and* stand out. Others might have started doing heroin, say. That's a form of traumatic coping too. But me? I quietly stopped eating. I wanted people to notice because deep down I wanted help, but I also wanted to appear functional. It really fitted with who I was: a perfectionist who cared deeply about what other people thought. This perfectionist, who wanted people to like and approve of her, was never going to shoot up. My coping strategy reflected my upbringing and personality, but what I've learnt is that they're both crutches, both addictions, both ways of avoiding our pain.

There are three main types of *high* from repetitively using a process or substance: arousal, satiation and deprivation.[2] All three types of high make us feel above our pain and anxiety.

- The *arousal* high comes from the first few giddy drinks of alcohol, drugs that ramp us up, such as amphetamines and ecstasy, gambling, sex, spending, stealing. It causes sensations of intense, raw, unchecked power and gives us the feeling of being untouchable and all-powerful.

- The *satiation* high comes from things like over-eating, binge-drinking, Valium, binge-watching TV, heroin or playing slot machines. All these kinds of substances and processes give us the feeling of being full, whole, soothed or numb.
- The *deprivation* high comes from going without food, without spending money, without sex or intimacy. It makes us feel in control and ready for the worst, and enables us to control our rising terror.

The Addictive Personality by Craig Nakken is one of the classic texts on addiction and recovery.[3] In it he explains that at the top level, seeking a high is all about seeking a mood change. These mood changes bring us into a kind of *trance* that detaches us from our pain, anxiety, guilt and shame. Nakken's explanation of why we seek this trance-like state has been burnt into my mind since reading it more than fifteen years ago.

Nakken explains that addictive patterns aren't just about avoiding pain, they're about chasing a deep, meaningful sense of connection.[4] We lean on our crutch because we want to feel *more* connected, *more* whole, *more* intimate, *more* spiritual. But the connection we experience is an illusion. We connect to a thing or a process for this sense of wholeness, but in doing so we further disconnect from our body, our feelings, our core, our adult self, all that is universal and essential, from other people and from the world.

What I desperately needed was wholeness, connection and intimacy, but my resistance to sitting with and owning my pain pushed these things further and further away.

Whether you relate to what I'm saying here, as I describe addictive processes, or whether you're certain addiction is not relevant to you, we're all aiming for the same thing. We all need to live in a way that allows us to stay with our feelings rather than push them away. Hard if the feelings are overwhelming, as they often can be if we've experienced trauma. But it's something we need to learn over time. We slowly shift, with the help of therapists if need be, into a state of recognising, feeling and owning our feelings. We learn to stop reaching for something *out there* every time we feel something *in here*. Our honesty and increasing ability to tolerate our feelings enables us to break out of the loops we're stuck in, reconnect with our body, core and adult self and reclaim our life.

Trauma and addiction

There's a lot of debate about the relationship between trauma and addiction, and how closely entwined the two are. Although I love that we're talking about trauma and addiction, I don't fully understand why it gets so complicated. To me, it seem pretty clear: people experience trauma and try to cope with the triggered reactions and emotional pain by using certain substances or processes. We're also, as it turns out, hardwired to learn and develop habits, so once you start leaning heavily on a dysfunctional crutch you're setting yourself on a path. This path is dependency and then addiction. If you really commit, it's destruction and death.

Perhaps your crutch, your dysfunctional relationship with, say, food or alcohol, developed in direct response to your initial traumatic experience? Mine did, for sure. For this reason, and because no one realised that the sudden onset of my eating disorder was a traumatic reaction, this coping mechanism was given the time and space it needed to really set in. My traumatic coping bedded down and took over. It became a deeply ingrained habit, a go-to crutch of the highest order. It helped me cope with my pain *and* it created its own set of problems. This is the truth of all dysfunction – if you catch it early, if you recognise that the dysfunctional crutch has developed in response to trauma, it can be corrected. With support, honesty and work, it can be sent on its merry way. If a crutch is given the time and space it needs to really take hold, it's hard to pull back from it. This book is about change and growth, so what I've just said may sound a little out-of-step, a little too negative.

If a crutch is given the time and space it needs to really take hold, it's hard to pull back from it.

This is the truth. It's hard to row back from decades of dysfunctional traumatic coping. Even today, if I'm triggered I sometimes feel the call to not eat. It's a pull, a compulsion.

Deep down in my subconscious, thirteen-year-old Sarah says: *this will feel better if you restrict; if you're thin you'll have that at least; you don't deserve to eat; you don't deserve love.* I don't hear the words, but I feel them.

If you've experienced trauma you're likely to have a main go-to crutch. Like mine, it will call to you when you're triggered. I'm not saying your crutch is food. Maybe it's alcohol, shopping, overworking, prescription drugs, cocaine, people-pleasing, codependency, compulsively cleaning the house, avoiding people. Maybe it's not dysfunctional, though? Maybe it's journalling, calling someone you trust and venting, polyvagal breathing, yoga or emotional release. I hope it is one of these kinds of empowering strategies that help you break the loop. But for many, it's likely to be the kind of crutch that keeps us trapped and repeating – as mine did.

Now, if I'm triggered, these are the things I do. I'll observe the trigger and my reactions; I'll voice my feelings. I'll ground myself. I'll seek healthy, human connection. I'll make the choice to still eat dinner. Then I'll eat. That's the difference; that's the growth. That's how I change the pattern and break the loop. It's a daily choice that no longer feels like a struggle. Yes, if you allow a crutch to imprint on the mind, body and spirit, it's hard to row back from. Hard, but not impossible. The other side, out of the loop, out of the struggle to break the habit, is freedom. Freedom from the crutch itself and freedom from all the reactive emotions, thoughts and beliefs that go with it. And it's worth all the effort.

Booze

Alcohol is really addictive. Perhaps you have a little smile on your face because of the simplicity of what I've just said. You already know this? Okay, but do you really *get* it? Consuming a substance like alcohol can quickly turn into a dependency, and this dependency can smoothly and easily transform into an addiction.

Think of Pavlov's dog. You know this classical conditioning experiment, right? Pavlov presented his dog with a stimulus – the sound of a metronome – and then gave the dog food. After a few repetitions, the dog started to salivate in response to the sound of the metronome. Booze, like dog food, becomes easily associated with a stimulus. Could having a beer be associated in your mind with the sound of a metronome?! More likely, it's associated with being in a pub, seeing certain friends, feeling certain feelings. You want a drink to relax after work? Pavlov's dog. Gin and tonic after the kids go to bed? Pavlov's dog. You always fancy a cold beer or glass of white wine when it's sunny? Pavlov's dog.

Alcohol can be joyful and spontaneous. But it's also easy to develop a dependency to it. Depending on your pattern of drinking, you may not be responding to life and situations in a fluid and *free* way. If this sounds like you, you're not saying *yes* to a glass of wine because you happen to fancy it. You're saying *yes* because that's how you've programmed your brain and body. It's a pattern; a dependency. Breaking the pattern is critical if you want to live a free, spontaneous life and connect to your true feelings.

Take a month off booze and see what happens. Go out for dinner with your friends without drinking. Friday night's drinking night? Don't drink. See what happens, see what comes up. If these kinds of choices feel consistently easy, it's unlikely there's a dependency. If these choices feel hard; if there's a lengthy internal dialogue; if there's huge resistance; if there's a preoccupation with the choice you've made, or alcohol itself, there may be an issue you need to address.

This is especially relevant if you've experienced trauma. We all need to be honest and open about whether our feelings and triggers have become associated with alcohol. If you pick up a drink every time you're triggered, you've developed a dependency. As I've said, many people who experience trauma develop addictions to help them cope, so you need to be very real and very honest as you consider your relationship with alcohol.

If alcohol is a crutch for you and this is the first time you've really started to own this fact, you might be about to dive into a month or so of proving to yourself that you're *not* an alcoholic. As you contemplate this, please know that there's no shame in it. It's not a moral issue. Being an alcoholic isn't wrong. It's not a sign of failure. It simply means you're a human, with a story to tell. Being a *recovered* alcoholic is a badge of honour. Some of the most enlightened, spiritual, healthy, open, loving people I know are recovered alcoholics and addicts. Overcoming adversity and trauma leads to greatness. Adversity and trauma also lead to addiction so, go figure, many of the greats are also recovering addicts.

People go to Alcoholics Anonymous (AA), or a similar program, when they realise they can't control the dependency or addiction on their own – that willpower isn't enough. Don't get me wrong, I'm not of the belief that the fellowships (e.g. AA, Over-eaters Anonymous, Narcotics Anonymous, Co-Dependents Anonymous, Sex and Love Addicts Anonymous, Al-Anon, etc.) are the only way to heal addiction and compulsion. But I definitely am of the belief that recovery from dysfunctional coping is not a road we can walk alone.

Halt . . . then find your people

Although I said I wasn't going to go into detail about triggers, there's one phrase I want to tell you. When I was very new to eating disorder recovery, an older woman, who'd been recovering and thriving for over thirty years, said this to me: 'When you're hungry, angry, lonely, or tired, your recovery is going to feel really hard.'

This simple statement is still true today. Hunger, Anger, Loneliness and Tiredness can all trigger my traumatic coping. Imagine what a bumpy road new motherhood was with this last little trigger! Tired?! Yes much! What this acronym (HALT) reminds us is that life is hard, and when it gets hard, you're going to want to fall back on your crutch. This is fine if your crutch is empowering, but not great if your crutch is disempowering and dysfunctional. These difficult parts of life are often triggers for trauma and addiction. They drive us into a space where our prefrontal cortex (the part of our brain responsible for planning, decision-making and self-control) takes a backseat. They can pull us back into the loops we're trying to break out of. I mentioned anger and loneliness in the previous chapters, but our physical triggers also need to be laid bare. Hunger. Tiredness. Stress. Physical pain. Who can think straight in these states? Very few people! So understand now, as you move forward, that when you're under-resourced and low in energy, things are going to get very real. Honouring the process of breaking free will feel difficult. It's on these days that your dysfunctional crutch is going to stretch out its arms and offer you a cuddle. Saying yes to it would feel like putting on your favourite fluffy pyjamas. Saying no to it will take strength and courage. It may be hard to do it alone.

On these days, when it feels hard, and difficult old feelings surface, you're going to need the support of some healthy, respectful, loving, *recovered* people. Perhaps these people are in a 12-step meeting, perhaps they're a local support group. Perhaps it's an online community. Perhaps it's your partner, perhaps it's your friends. Perhaps it's your family. Whoever these people are, the relationships need to be respectful and loving. The relationships need to be honest and open, with healthy boundaries. The people you lean on need to be taking personal responsibility for their own feelings and actions (i.e. not ignoring their own active addictions or rampant unhealed trauma). The people you trust with your growth need to reflect the future you want. Breaking old loops means shifting into the new. Only people who empower you should be invited along for the ride.

In the previous chapter I said relationships are hard work. This is true. But connecting to empowering, respectful, loving people who are taking responsibility for their own lives and healing will help you reprogram your mind and body. People are hard work, but they're also the solution.

The mind–body connection

Our feelings are experienced in our body. Maybe we feel it in our tummy, our chest, our throat. Think about anxiety, for example. What does it feel like when you're anxious? For me, it's all up in my chest. I'm tense in the rest of my body, but the main to-do is up high. I can't catch my breath. My chest and shoulders feel simultaneously heavy and tingly. My heart flutters. There are other things going on in my mind and with my emotions, but let's stay focused on the body for now. Anxiety and fear are experienced physically. Anger and shame are experienced physically. Excitement? Joy? These are all *felt*. Where? The body. I get that this is simple, but have you ever really engaged with the fact feelings are experienced physically?! For some dumb-founding reason we don't explain to children that feelings are *felt* in the body. We tell them what they're called, but we don't help them discover what they feel like as physical sensations.

I'm mentioning this to illustrate one of the cruel paradoxes of trauma. Trauma involves overwhelming emotions, like fear, threat or shame, all of which are experienced where? All together now: the body. But despite the very physical

132

nature of trauma, many of us are unable to properly connect with, and feel at one with our body. At the very time we need to be most in touch with our physical body, to help us understand our feelings and process them, we disconnect.

There are many reasons we disconnect from our body, some of which I mentioned in chapter three as I described the Trauma Loop (pp. 68 to 69). For one, the traumatic reaction itself actually encourages it. Think about dissociation. This common response to trauma leads to us feeling spaced out and separate not just from the world around us, but from our body. Many aspects of the traumatic reaction are trying to protect us from an emotional pain it thinks we can't bear. This is why learning to sit with our emotions and notice our physical sensations is such a critical part of trauma healing. Every time we can stay with an uncomfortable feeling, for even just one second longer than before, we teach ourselves that we can bear it – that we don't have to keep running away. When this is coupled with us paying greater attention to the good feelings too (e.g. the warmth of the sun on our skin), we begin a new relationship with our body and encourage healing.

Do you remember the story I told in the introduction, about how I intellectualised the 'trauma problem' the therapist posed to me? This story sums up another reason we gradually disconnect from our body: we retreat into the mind. Our body is our home and should be a place of safety and support. Traumatic reactions make our *home* feel uninhabitable, so many of us retreat into the mind. But the mind is reliant on the body for information, instinct and guidance.

It needs the body to calm it and ground it, and bring it back to the here and now. When the mind is disconnected from the body, it can cause us no end of problems.

I remember someone referring to their mind as 'an ego-manic child, screaming orders and hell-bent on self-destruction.' How could I forget that! She perfectly describes how the mind can run riot if left to its own devices.

Healing from trauma is about reconnecting the mind and the body. Many of us shift from a life where we ignore our body's sensations, instincts and needs to a life where our body is lovingly allowed to take the lead. As we heal, our mind is taught to pause. Our thoughts are no longer given free rein. Our thinking makes way for our feelings, and our mind makes way for our body.

Our body is constantly changing and looking for ways to heal. If we can rein in the mind, and gently develop a new relationship with our body, we can create new neural pathways within our nervous system. Here, as I talk about new neural pathways, I'm referring to neuroplasticity, the ability of the nervous system to change and adapt.[5] This glorious body of research is pure hope! It demonstrates that our nervous system will respond to the positive changes that we make. The overarching message: we can heal.

Physical health and wellbeing

Because trauma is such a physical experience, it can greatly affect health and wellbeing. Many people living with trauma do not *feel* well. They report living with very low energy levels, and often feel rundown or swing between very high energy levels one day to very low energy levels the next. This is a result of our dysregulated nervous system and the toll it takes on our body. Others, as you'll read later in this section, report more specific, medical issues – chronic pain or autoimmune issues, for example.

In the previous chapters, I've mentioned our growing understanding of how trauma affects our physical health. This is a complicated topic and one that requires its own book, so here I'm just giving a whistle-stop tour. If you're interested in going deeper into this area I highly recommend Dr Nadine Burke Harris's book *Toxic Childhood Stress*.[6] Somatic theories also help explain the link between trauma and physical health, so Peter Levine's *In an Unspoken Voice*[7] is also an excellent read.

Between 1995 and 1997, a large US study called the Adverse Childhood Experiences (ACE) study[8] examined the relationship between difficult childhood experiences and long-term health in 17,500 people. It identified ten Adverse Childhood Experiences (ACEs), many of which are also on the big-T trauma list (p. 32):

- Emotional abuse (recurrent)
- Physical abuse (recurrent)
- Sexual abuse (involving contact/touch)
- Physical neglect (e.g. not having enough to eat)
- Emotional neglect (e.g. feeling unloved)
- Substance abuse in the household (e.g. living with someone with a drinking problem)

- Mental illness in the household (e.g. living with someone who suffered from depression, mental illness or someone who has attempted suicide)
- Mother treated violently
- Divorce or parental separation
- Criminal behaviour in household (e.g. a household member going to prison).

Sixty-seven per cent of those surveyed had experienced at least one of these ACEs. Thirteen per cent had experienced four or more. Dr Burke Harris rightly points out that 70 per cent of those surveyed were college-educated (meaning that the sample was mostly middle-class).[9] These were ordinary people, leading typical middle-America lives. There were many incredible findings from this study. Below are the ones relating to physical health that really blew my mind.

The study found that having an ACE score of four or more (i.e. having experienced four or more of the experiences listed above) roughly doubles a person's chance of developing the following chronic illnesses, compared to someone who has experienced no ACEs:

- developing heart disease
- having a stroke
- becoming obese or being very overweight
- getting any type of cancer.

Additionally, if a person has an ACE score of just two or more, it more than doubles someone's chance of developing an autoimmune disease.

Only 50 per cent of this increased risk factor could be accounted for by the person's behavioural and lifestyle factors (e.g. smoking, physical inactivity). The other 50 per cent is unaccounted for and still has psychologists and medics scratching their heads. Dr Burke Harris attributes these astonishing findings to the long-term effects of traumatic stress (she calls it 'toxic stress') on the body.

Here's a bare-bones explanation of how traumatic stress can lead to long-term health issues:

If we experience a prolonged traumatic reaction, over time our amygdala (the part of the brain responsible for emotions, survival and memory) becomes hypersensitive. We develop a state of high alert, reacting (overreacting) to everyday experiences as if they're a threat. This leads to an overactive nervous system, with too much cortisol, adrenaline and noradrenaline pumping around. If left elevated over time, these stress hormones can negatively affect our brain structure and function, our other hormones and our immune system. Over time, because of these changes, we're more likely to experience difficult physical symptoms and diagnoses (like those listed above).

The physical health outcomes the ACE study found to be associated with previous trauma and adversity are far from psychosomatic. These are very real physical issues that appear to relate back to an overactive amygdala, Hypothalamic–Pituitary–Adrenal (HPA) axis and other aspects of our autonomic nervous system. (For a detailed explanation of these terms, please refer to the glossary at the end of the book.) This is why so many people say trauma becomes *trapped* in the body.

If you've been living with this heightened stress – responding to every threat, conflict or loud bang as if you're tooling up and going into battle – it's likely that your body has suffered. And this isn't just about the life-threatening outcomes the original ACE study focused on, it's about everyday pain and tension. It's about the outcomes I listed in the introduction: migraines and headaches, back ache, premenstrual tension and chronic pain.[10]

Although researchers are still trying to ascertain the precise causal mechanisms at work, the evidence has become indisputable. I'm so grateful to the researchers and the somatic psychotherapists working in this field – people dedicated to understanding and healing the physical manifestations of trauma. Their work has showed us that trauma can damage our health in broad, systemic, debilitating ways. Individually and collectively, we all need to take this seriously.

Chapter Six

How trauma affects your work and education

Whenever I talk about trauma (which is often), work and education are the topics people get really pumped about. Most people haven't considered how their past trauma could affect their work or earning potential, so when I mention it, their eyes light up.

In part, this is because people haven't given it much thought before. But it's also because, for many people, work feels like a lighter, safer subject than love, sex, friendship, marriage, families, food, alcohol and physical health. In talking about this topic with people, I've come to realise that it's inherently solution-focused, and can become a source of hope for people. Because what we're talking about, really, is *potential*. As we move towards the final part of the book, this is exactly where I want us to be: considering what's possible. This isn't just about recovery – it's about living within your *power*, not living in powerlessness. It's this topic that allows people to see their potential for transformation.

The survival response at work

All types of employment and most learning environments involve us delivering outcomes to someone higher up the pecking order. There's an expectation that work will be completed on time and to a certain standard. Often, this leads to a sense of pressure and stress. On top of this, most types of employment and learning involve working with other people, collaborating or being part of a team. This entails complicated interpersonal interactions, discussions, compromise, criticism and conflict resolution. And then there's the very real fact that most people work to earn money so they can eat, pay the rent and buy what they need. As well as supporting themselves, many people are also supporting a family, paying a mortgage, paying school fees or planning a house renovation. Most people are building a life that requires them not just to keep their job, but to excel at their job and earn more money as their career progresses. No pressure there!

As a trauma researcher I'm fascinated by people's work environments because, as you may have picked up, they can be a breeding ground for triggered traumatic reactions. The hierarchies, power dynamics, pressure, stress, conflict, criticism, expectations and the overarching need to keep the job. Of course, it's inherently about survival. There's a need to get it right to ensure we can first meet our basic needs, then keep moving up the pecking order.

I get that work can also be deeply fulfilling, fun, creative, exciting, satisfying, joyful and many other important, useful things. But it can also sometimes be a difficult context to operate within. Work, as I described above, involves many potentially triggering situations. Once the fight, flight, freeze response is triggered, we're in survival mode and, as you've learnt, this space is not conducive to clear thinking, let alone producing great work.

Work and higher education can, and should, be fulfilling. They should be a source of satisfaction and joy in our lives (most of the time, at least). When it isn't like this – if instead it's uncomfortable and unsatisfying – people tend to look for big-ticket, quick-fix solutions. They change jobs, change careers or retrain. I did this so many times. Instead of taking each uncomfortable situation as an opportunity to grow, I bailed. Instead of spotting the patterns, joining the dots and observing the common denominators, I left. Sometimes I blamed others; more often I blamed myself. Either way, instead of staying still and learning, I ran. Can you relate to this? Perhaps, perhaps not. I've met just as many people who have the opposite reaction. People who stick and stick and stick in uncomfortable situations that aren't working for them. They epitomise the idea that work should feel hard. They're paying penance. Whether you bail and look for a quick fix or you stick until your eyes are bleeding, you're not learning what you need to learn. You're not growing. You're not empowered and owning your past, present or future. You're not taking responsibility for your success.

Triggered beliefs

Unless you're very unwell with trauma symptoms or you're leaning very heavily on a dysfunctional crutch (e.g. alcoholism), the principal way trauma will affect your education, career and ability to earn money is through your negative beliefs and cognitions. Yes, there may be other mechanisms at work, but in my experience it's the self-defeating, deeply ingrained, negative beliefs about ourselves and the world that interfere the most. Likewise, of course, the reverse of this is true. People who have positive, empowering beliefs – *I can do anything, mistakes are how I learn, I will succeed, I am capable, I will earn a high salary, I deserve respect, I am a leader* – are in the best position to thrive in the workplace.

All work environments involve potentially triggering situations. Unprocessed traumatic memories are easily tripped. When they are, you're thrown back into childhood or early adulthood. The assertive, confident, empowered you disappears and in comes the smaller, younger, frightened, reactive you. The negative cognitions and beliefs may also be accompanied by an overwhelming feeling, perhaps shame, anger or fear. Perhaps physical sensations like anxiety, a racing heart, dizziness, dissociation or spacing out also come along for the ride. It's not just about the cognitions, but in the context of work this is what we really need to focus on.

Take Anna. She had a high-pressure graduate accounting job which she had worked incredibly hard to get. Aside from the fact she was almost permanently anxious (which in itself is a big red flag), Anna's friends and family often commented to her that she 'took criticism at work too personally'. They were right: Anna did take criticism at work too personally. Anna worked at one of the top international accounting firms. The culture was very competitive, and those in the graduate roles were used to honest feedback if they made a mistake or didn't perform. After presenting at a client meeting, Anna was reprimanded in front of her team for not being assertive enough. Her boss didn't lose it at her – she was measured but firm, and very clear that Anna had not performed well enough. After the dressing-down, Anna sat down at her desk. Her overwhelming, all-encompassing sense was: *I'm a failure*. Two weeks later, she was called into her boss's office because she'd been underperforming and behaving unusually. Anna's boss pointed out that she had become shut down, distracted and cripplingly indecisive, and that she had isolated herself from her team. Her boss didn't say, 'I think your childhood trauma was triggered when I criticised you', because she didn't know that Anna had been triggered, and neither did Anna, but that's what had happened.

Being criticised is a common trigger for many people. Anna's response was fairly typical of a freeze response: shut down, avoid, pull back, space out. Others will have more of a flight response: high anxiety, compulsive busyness, perfectionism, worrying. Some will have more of a fight response – aggression, conflict, defensiveness. Or some, like me, move through a combination of two or more responses.

Being criticised can, and should, happen at work. It should be done constructively and kindly, but we only grow when we're called out on our mistakes. We only learn and

143

thrive when we're held accountable. If we want to succeed, we have to learn how to control our triggered reactions, so we can learn the lessons we need to allow us to grow. If we walk out and shut down, dive into perfectionism and obsessive worry or become defensive and aggressive, we will never learn. We'll remain stuck. We'll remain in an old pattern, trapped in an old loop.

For Anna, being harshly criticised by her mother was a frequent event during her childhood. This led to a solid (although incorrect and self-defeating) belief that she was a failure. This triggered belief frequently interfered with her work at critical moments. It undermined her and her career until many years later when she did her trauma work and moved past it.

It's not just criticism that can trigger us. Take Kyle, for whom not getting a promotion at work triggered a huge fight response (he angrily handed in his notice). This traumatic (over)reaction was connected to one main negative belief: *I'm stupid.* Not getting the promotion subconsciously proved to Kyle that he was stupid. The belief was triggered, along with his fight response, and he walked out of a job he was doing well at. It turned out that Kyle had come to this painful conclusion as a child one evening at his grandfather's house, when he couldn't catch a ball his grandfather threw to him. While laughing, his grandfather said, 'You really are a stupid little bugger,' threw the ball at the ground and walked off. Kyle had other trauma, so his fight response didn't just stem from this one incident, but the belief that was triggered related to the experience with his grandfather when he was seven years old.

Despite the fact that the initial traumatic experience is always a negative experience, the *trigger* itself doesn't have to be. The trigger may not always be a criticism, a conflict, a difficult boss, a lost promotion or a lost client. For example, Mark was asked to do an important presentation at work for one of his employer's major clients. It was a big pat on the back, but he immediately became extremely anxious and concerned about his ability to do it. When I asked him what was going on, he was incredibly clear. He said, 'I can't handle the pressure. It's hard to believe I have what it takes; I'm sure I'll drop the ball.' These low self-beliefs had grown from his experiences at a tough all-boys secondary school, where he was frequently criticised and put down by other pupils and certain staff members.

Time and time again I speak with people who are triggered by something good: an opportunity, praise, a sale, an invitation, a promotion. Why? Because the good news, and the projected sense of expectation that comes with it, can trigger our old traumatic beliefs. What if I fail? What if I'm not good enough? What if I can't perform? What do they expect from me? These subconscious reactions to positive opportunities and feedback are common, and they cause considerable damage. Many walk away or sabotage their own success to avoid the imagined possibility of failure, disappointment and pain.

Below is a list of traumatic cognitions that can be triggered in a work context. I've heard them many times, repeated in many different forms over the years. I've included some work-related cognitions uncovered by Dr Francine Shapiro during her thirty years of research and practice into unprocessed traumatic memory.[1] She helpfully groups them into three categories: lack of control and power, being defective, and lack of safety. Some of these cognitions were highlighted in chapter one. In the context of education, work and money, you can see how damaging they are when they're triggered:

Lack of control and power
I'm a failure
I cannot succeed
I have to be perfect
I can't handle it
I'm powerless (helpless)
I cannot get what I want
I cannot stand up for myself
I cannot trust myself

Being defective
I'm a disappointment
I'm stupid
I'm worthless
I'm not enough
I have nothing to offer
I'm permanently damaged
I do not deserve respect

Lack of safety
It's not safe to show my emotions

It's not safe to assert myself
It's not safe unless I'm in charge
I'm not safe unless I get what I want
It's not safe to make mistakes.

The flavour of these types of negative cognitions is always the same. Always a final, fundamental, negative, shame-based conclusion about the self or the world. These types of negative cognitions derail us at the time we most need to be on track. It's important to point out that no one said to Mark that he couldn't handle it. Anna's boss didn't call her a failure. Kyle's boss didn't call him stupid. It's what they heard. It was the voice of the past.

No one at work is likely to call you a failure (I hope) but because of, say, their tone of voice, it's what you'll hear. It's unfair on you, and usually it's unfair on the other person. Being triggered makes us draw the same self-hating, negative conclusions we did at the time of the trauma. We then take these conclusions as fact. We evidence-gather (*I didn't get the promotion*) to prove that our misguided traumatic cognitive reactions are correct (*therefore I'm stupid*). Not only do we need to learn to step back from triggers, we also need to learn to fact-check. *My boss didn't actually say I'm stupid; maybe I need a conversation with her about why she decided not to give me the promotion this time.*

I can see my negative beliefs there winking at me in the list above. Honestly, in relation to my business and work, they're still triggered sometimes. In fact, it seems that the further I go in my career, the more these guys like to show up and try to derail me. The difference is, now I don't give them any power over me. I feel the trigger, I observe the reaction, I fact-check, and reconnect with my core and my adult self today. This is the process we all need to learn to ensure we thrive in our careers.

Groundhog day

Trauma is intrinsically about repetition, so one way to establish when and how we're triggered is to look for the negative repetitions and patterns in our life. This applies to relationships and our health. But it also applies to our education, our career and our relationship with money. If we look for the negative situations that keep coming back, we're likely to find a trigger that pushes us into a physical, emotional, cognitive and behavioural loop. Keep looking and we often find the initial trauma at the base of it.

Nick's working life is an example of these kinds of blindingly-obvious-once-you-know repetitions. Nick was thirty-five years old when I met him. He was doing well at work, but time and time again found himself in conflict with the males he worked with. No matter the job, no matter the culture at work, Nick always ended up in a dispute with a male colleague. Not the women, just the men. It caused him (and others) tension and stress, and on more than one occasion these conflicts led to him leaving a job. Nick couldn't feel this in the moment when he was triggered, but he figured it out because of the pattern. The repetition of the situation (in total, this occurred over ten times) allowed him to observe the pattern and find the trigger. In Nick's case, the trigger was always a male speaking to him in what he considered to be a patronising tone of voice. It triggered unprocessed traumatic childhood memories of his aggressive, overbearing father, and sent him into a fight response (literally fighting, albeit verbally).

Or, take Eva. Eva was on fire. Not literally, but in terms of her working life and bank balance they were all moving forward at tremendous speed. BMW: tick. Big house: tick. Holiday home: tick. Externally, she appeared to have it all. But she was stressed and lonely. This was her pattern: she took promotions or applied for new jobs that came with a lot more work and a lot more money. She did this despite the fact that she was stressed and had no life outside of work. Her work was no longer making her happy, but she kept on moving up an imaginary ladder. Part of her wanted to stop, but she couldn't. She realised, eventually, that the thing she had been doing (working harder and harder despite wanting to slow down) was driven by trauma from her relationship with her father.

Like many people, Eva was desperate for validation from her father. He was an impossible man to please, and reacted with little interest in Eva's success. She went into her career in television to please him, and she still slogged it out twenty years later because of him. He was either mildly dismissive or actively rude about her choices. Nonetheless, Eva kept trying, in the hope that one day he'd say he was proud of her. Even though it seems obvious as I describe it retrospectively, Eva wasn't aware of her subconscious traumatic motivation. It was only when she looked at her life pattern, which eventually she was forced to do because of a distressing breakup with a partner, that she saw the repetition and the trauma response.

I've chosen to tell you about Eva because if you saw her, with her beautiful clothes and confidence, you would think she was living her best life. But she was motivated by a subconscious belief that she was worthless. Realising that this belief was at work was devastating for Eva, and the realisation came with a lot of grief. But it also propelled her into healing and into doing her trauma work. She connected to her core, found her own motivation and a new path through life.

Many personal development books and life coaches mention these types of *self-limiting beliefs*. The types of beliefs that get in the way of our careers, happiness or earning potential. Not all self-limiting beliefs stem from trauma. Some seep in from society at large as we watch how the world works (e.g. women don't talk about our accomplishments, but men do), others from our parents (e.g. creative professions aren't a reliable source of income). As we think about our self-limiting beliefs and where they've led us, it's useful to consider which beliefs are traumatic. It's a subtle but important shift in thinking. It allows us to really understand the processes at work. Traumatic beliefs are fuelled by the fight, flight, freeze response. They're the outcome of our overwhelming response to a perceived threat and often link to a deeper sense of powerlessness or helplessness. Applying a trauma model explains the belief, the repetition of the belief, and the feelings and behaviours that accompany the belief. Applying a trauma model explains why we get stuck, and it gives us a model and pathway to get unstuck.

Self-esteem

Self-esteem is defined as confidence in our own worth or ability. It is our appraisal and analysis of us. Confidence is a felt experience, but at the base of confidence are the conclusions we've drawn about ourselves over the years. These are the beliefs I've been banging on about for six chapters.

Can I do it? Am I smart enough? Will it be okay? Do I have it in me? Can I run a successful business? Should I take a risk in my career? Do I have anything to give? Should I charge for my expertise? Can I do the job? Should I go for the promotion? When we ask ourselves questions like these, our fundamental self-beliefs answer them before we've had a chance to fact-check. This is fine if our fundamental self-belief is that we rock. Can I run a successful business? Hell yes! Will it be okay? Sure it will! Should I charge for my expertise? OF COURSE!

Great answers, based on secure, confident self-beliefs. And now, the reality for those living with trauma:

Can I run a successful business? You're an idiot for even asking the question. Will it be okay? No, it never is. Should I charge for my expertise? Your opinion is worthless, so OF COURSE NOT.

What I'm highlighting here is that our trauma-led negative beliefs are at play more broadly than when we're reminded of the initial trauma. Over time, they lead to a negative sense of self and low self-esteem, both of which are relevant across many situations. If your sense of self is built on any of those final, fundamental, negative beliefs that I listed, it's highly likely that you have low self-esteem – little confidence in your own ability or worth. Chances are you can't see yourself as you really are or see your full potential. Not at the moment. But as you do your work and reconnect to your core, you'll be able to see your true self in all its beauty.

Enough

I met Rachel at a conference in Spain. I was there talking about my research and she was there with a client of hers. Rachel worked in political lobbying, and given that I used to work in the same field, we hit it off. Most often I get one of two responses when I tell someone I research trauma. Either they look confused and check out, or they light up and I can tell they have a story. The thing about trauma is that it's an inherently human issue. Rachel had the second response, so I knew there was a story coming. As we sat in a little café at dusk, with a beautiful view of the Alhambra in Granada, she told me her incredible, inspiring story of moving from trauma to transformation.

'I moved to London after university, and I immediately loved it,' she said. 'I was single, living in a beautiful apartment and had a great graduate job. Life felt good! You know that feeling, when you think you can do anything?'

I laughed and said, 'Yes, I know that feeling! I love that feeling – that's THE feeling!'

'Exactly,' she said, 'and it felt so good because I'd never felt like that before. Life before I moved there was hard. I had always felt like a failure. I was embarrassed to be me, you know? I was self-conscious, confused and afraid. I felt like I got everything wrong and had nothing to offer. But then it all shifted when I moved to London.'

Rachel proceeded to tell me her story – how she was sexually assaulted in the washroom of a bar one evening. And how, in that moment, everything changed. She told me how small her life became after that evening. Her job, which had been going so well, started to go wrong. Her work required her to be enthusiastic and energetic. It also required her to socialise – to engage in conversation, to negotiate and build relationships. It often required her to be out in the evening, with people (often men) who were eager to talk to her. What she could once hold lightly and with joy felt unsafe, sordid and impossible.

'What happened in the bar proved to me, 100 per cent, that I was a failure. It proved to me that I would amount to nothing. It proved to me that I was a naive idiot for thinking I could be anything at all.'

What she said has always stayed with me. As I think about her now, I engage fully with why I'm writing this book. What do you hear in Rachel's words? I hear shame, self-blame, powerlessness and fear. I hear negative, traumatic beliefs.

I chose to tell you about Rachel because the contrast is so stark. As she left university and travelled to London she stepped out of her past and into her power, only to be brutally thrown back into her old beliefs and feelings. But the truth is – and I think you understand trauma well enough now to know this – what happened that night in the bar was not her *first* trauma. The feelings she felt after the experience in the bar were not actually new at all. She had felt it all before; she had been operating within these beliefs her whole life. That she was a failure. That she would amount to nothing. Hidden fears and beliefs, shame and low self-esteem, all of which prevented her from stepping into her power. And the minute she did step forward? She was slammed back down.

'I had an appraisal at work and, of course, it went terribly,' she explained. 'My boss told me about all the negative feedback she was receiving about me from clients, and how disappointed she was by my recent lack of enthusiasm. She said that when I first took the job, she had felt sure I would end up directing the team one day, and that she was genuinely surprised by how things were going.

'The conversation with my boss was my turning point. I walked out of there and I just said – *enough*. It seemed like a very clear choice to me: I either let the experience destroy my career and me, or I reclaim my life.

'I didn't know I was strong, but I just felt this huge sense of power. It was like something inside me was roaring. This light came back on. I felt clear and I felt strong.'

Rachel told me about the psychotherapeutic work she embarked on, and the amazing people she'd met as a result

of doing this work. She told me how she came to understand that her initial trauma was a physical assault she
experienced at about seven years old.

'As part of all the conversations and healing, I realised
how I'd been living this half-life, with my self-esteem on
the floor because of what had happened when I was seven.
It used to feel like my mind was trying to destroy me –
telling me I was a failure, telling me I would amount to
nothing.

'I get that I was handed this shame by other people, but
I also had to really own the fact that the voice telling me
I was shit was my own. I had to take back control and learn
to replace this voice with a kind one. As I did my work,
that's what happened.'

I will always, always remember this conversation with
Rachel, not least because of how eloquent and passionate
she was. She is the poster girl for moving from trauma to
transformation because, as we sat in this café, she proudly
told me that ten years after the incident in the bar, she
became director of her team. She loved her career, and
bravely facing her trauma had led her to meaningful, deep,
real transformation and success.

Over the years I've had many conversations with people
like Rachel – people who've made it clear to me that traumatic experiences affect our ability to own our power and
succeed. Of course they do, right? Trauma *is* powerlessness.
Trauma is shame. Trauma is negative, false, self-defeating
beliefs. Trauma is low self-esteem and self-hatred. Trauma
is denial and hiding parts of ourselves.

Just as Rachel did, we all have to roar in its face. We all need that moment – just as she experienced in her appraisal with her boss – where we say *enough*. Enough to the powerlessness, shame and self-hatred.

Enough.

The wrong path

My explanation of trauma in chapter one includes the survival response, unprocessed memories and cyclical loops. As I've illustrated, all these different aspects of trauma can affect our education, work and money. But there was a last part to the definition too, remember?

Trauma is our disconnection from our sense of self, others and the world that follows the traumatic experience.

Of all the four parts of our explanation of trauma, I think this one immediately shouts out its own relevance to the topics we're discussing here. To ensure we're on the right life path – one that feels authentic and allows us to reach our potential – we have to be connected to our body, our core and ourselves. To make great, empowered decisions about our own education and careers, we need to be able to take a beat, take a breath, and connect to the part of us that knows the way. We need to be awake, conscious and honest.

By living this way, we're able to own our mistakes as well as our successes, because they came from choices we made in a conscious and empowered way. Disconnection from self leads to us disowning our mistakes because we don't feel that *we* made them. It breeds shame, defensiveness, blame, fear and anger. Disconnection from self leads to a surreal sense that we're pulled from left to right like a leaf in the wind. We jump, we react, we're triggered. Connection to our core allows us to know when *we're* making a decision or when something else is at work. Think of Eva. She didn't know something else was at work, because she was disconnected and reacting. As she reconnected, she reclaimed her life.

I've learnt this the hard way. I was cripplingly detached from my core, so I made fearful choices based on what I thought I *should* do. Two reactions drove my decisions around my education and work – fear and people-pleasing. I was either anxious and dissociated or trying to second guess what other people would think of my choices. I didn't engage with what I wanted or needed. I didn't connect with myself, because I couldn't. There was no instinct, no internal guidance, no calm connection to my highest self. I ran fearfully and erratically towards a version of success that wasn't mine. The mechanism was so quick, so habitual, that a less honest person wouldn't have to own it, even now. I could keep pretending, if I wanted to.

This story illustrates it perfectly. I was nineteen years old and travelling in Cambodia with my dearest friends. I was on a gap year and when I returned to the UK I was going to start an undergraduate degree in graphic design. I loved art and design and I was very good at it. Not only was it my passion, it was a healthy, loving choice for myself, as it required me to have a strong connection to my body and the present moment, and be creative. We arrived at a hostel on the banks of the Tonlé Sap Lake. After unpacking, we went down to the bar and, as you do when you're travelling, soon met a group of people. They were older than us and to me they seemed mysterious and wonderful. Halfway through the evening, one of the older women in the group said to me:

'So, what are you doing when you get back to the UK?'

'I'm starting a graphic design course,' I said, proudly.

She shot me a dismissive look, rolled her eyes, and said, 'Really? But you seem far too interesting to do graphic design.'

I remember this overwhelming feeling of embarrassment, confusion, fear and shame. She, and the rest of her friends, proceeded to discuss the merits of graphic design. Their dismissive (and drunk) conclusion was that the only truly useful things to study were politics, economics and journalism. I didn't hear what they said with objectivity or interest. I certainly didn't disagree with her (even though I do now). Instead, faced with someone belittling my choices, someone who I had subconsciously decided was 'better than me', I walked out on myself. I found myself agreeing with her completely. I felt ashamed of my choices and myself. I had felt this before and have felt it since. This rising, awful, panicked fear that I am not enough. A deep fear that someone doesn't *like* me and doesn't think I'm worthy of them. In these moments, I'm living within my child consciousness: I'm thirteen years old and back at school, afraid that people don't approve of me and are going to hurt me. I was all kinds of triggered and, worst of all, I had no idea that I was all kinds of triggered.

I emailed the university the next day and withdrew my place. I went all-in. I gave these strangers – who knew literally nothing about me – all my power. I did all this because I was triggered and thrown back into my traumatic thinking and beliefs. The decision I made that day took me away from a smaller campus college to a huge London one. It took me from art to journalism and, eventually, to politics. My ego, fear and people-pleasing grabbed onto strands of the *advice* I'd been given the night before and cobbled together a path for myself. In Cambodia I let go of my carefully considered path, and jumped into someone else's version of success.

What I didn't know at nineteen was that people often make the things we say about our own life about *them*. This older woman had a strong reaction to me doing graphic design. We could speculate about that. Was she triggered? Had she tried to get into a graphic design course and failed? Had her parents told her art was not a real subject? I'll never know, and it doesn't matter. What I do know is that just as I brought *me* to the table (and then totally walked out on myself), she brought herself (and all her own stuff). Now I see people's *stuff* as plainly as the nose on their face. I listen and I observe them, as well as me. I can hear real, grounded, objective advice and I can hear the opposite – misguided, egotistical, fear-led, triggered reactions.

Don't get me wrong, I now take full responsibility for the choices I made in Cambodia. But I also acknowledge that I was triggered. I acknowledge it to ensure that I learn from it, and to ensure it doesn't happen again. If we desert our self and disconnect, as we do when we're triggered, we run the risk of not only jumping on the wrong path, but never finding the right path in the first place. Our traumas are in the driver's seat.

To heal and grow, first we reconnect with our core, and then we see our path.

Part 3

How to break free and reclaim your life

Chapter Seven

What are growth and resilience?

Okay. Relax. Breathe easy. We made it to part three. Here we're going to look forward to the solution. Although it's not all unicorns and rainbows, there's no more heavy trauma chat. In this chapter, we're going to consider post-traumatic growth, spirituality, respectful relationships, resilience and the growth mindset (whatever that is!). So, admittedly, no unicorns but it's 100 per cent solution-focused.

Post-traumatic growth

Have you heard of post-traumatic growth? It's a beautiful concept and can be seen in millions of people around the world. Post-traumatic growth (PTG) describes people who experience trauma and then, in one way or another, thrive. People who don't take the traumatic experience as proof that they're damaged, but instead take it as proof that they're survivors. People who reconnect to their unbreakable core and higher self. People who build strong, resilient, positive identities in the face of great hardship and challenge. They rise up out of their reactions and patterns. The trauma itself becomes the motivation for growth and success. It puts fire in their belly and a determination not just to overcome, but to move forward into something beautiful. To transform.

This isn't just about the big names, well known for having overcome traumatic childhoods – people like Charlize Theron, Kelsey Grammer, Oprah Winfrey, Christina Aguilera and Curtis Jackson (50 Cent), who between them overcame abusive families, family tragedy, poverty, sexual assault and drugs. It's not just about people who live abundant lives of private jets and bejewelled swimming pools (I don't know if Oprah Winfrey has a bejewelled pool, but I'd like to think so!). This is about all kinds of people who transform from and through their trauma. Some – like the household names I've just mentioned – are so driven, so determined to rise above what they were handed, that they fly high and keep on going. The big names I've mentioned went all the way to the top despite their trauma. For others, it's about having joyful relationships despite carrying relational trauma. Feeling peace and contentment despite coming from chaotic, abusive families. Running a successful business. Feeling strong and self-assured. Being able to feel joy and happiness. The outcome isn't always tangible (e.g. that bejewelled swimming pool), but the outcome always involves positive transformation.

People who experience growth after a traumatic experience also experience overwhelm, self-doubt and fear. They also experience traumatic reactions. They may also be diagnosed with PTSD. They don't skip away from the traumatic experience with no traumatic reaction. They grow *despite* the traumatic reaction. This is what post-traumatic growth is – the extent to which someone experiences growth after trauma. I've grown. You've grown. Oprah Winfrey has grown, a lot. We can all grow more.

When growth after trauma is measured we ask how much people agree with statements such as:[1]

- I am better able to accept the way things work out.
- I can better appreciate each day.
- I can better accept needing others.
- I have a greater sense of closeness with others.
- I am more willing to express my emotions.
- I changed my priorities about what is important in life.
- I established a new path for my life.
- I am more likely to try to change things which need changing.
- I discovered that I'm stronger than I thought I was.
- I have a better understanding of spiritual matters.

People who strongly agree with these kinds of statements have high post-traumatic growth, so the statements tell us a lot about what we're aiming for. They show us that developing a greater appreciation for life and for ourselves; developing respectful, close relationships and being emotionally open with others; opening up to new possibilities and finding a new life path; recognising and reconnecting to our strength and exploring spiritual beliefs will help us transform through our trauma.

I'm fascinated by the post-traumatic growth research because it so clearly demonstrates how we can break free from trauma and thrive. And as you can see, this awesome area of research and theory supports so much of what I've been talking about in this book.

Spirituality

The last post-traumatic growth bullet point on the list above (p. 165) might stick in your throat if you're a devout atheist, so I think we should spend a moment considering what it means. Spirituality. Does the word carry a charge for you? Do you *react* to it with eye-rolling scorn? Did you react when I told the story of my experience at the ashram? There are, of course, many reasons someone might negatively react to the word *spirituality*. But here I'm talking to people who reacted because of their past trauma.

Traumatic experiences interfere with our ability to find meaning in life. The heartache, pain, mistrust and fear can strip us of our ability to connect with the idea that there's more to life than us. We can become nihilists of the highest order, believing in nothing. Of course, mistrust of spirituality doesn't always stem from trauma. It may be an active, thoughtful, considered position. But it might not be. It might be reactive and angry. It may have been handed to you by someone else, or based on conclusions you came to at a very difficult time in your life.

The dictionary defines spirituality as the quality of being concerned with the human spirit or soul as opposed to material or physical things.[2] But it's an impossible concept to fully define because it means different things to different people. For me, spirituality is about considering the connection between the self and the world. It means spending time considering the meaning of life. It means finding ways to connect with our deepest values, and looking inwards to consider what the *self* is. It also means looking outwards for connection, for something greater than ourselves. You don't have to be religious to experience spiritual growth. You don't have to believe in God. You just have to look for something greater than you – for meaning and connection.

No matter our stance on religion, souls, atheism, chakras, God, Om, universal energy, the Big Bang, paganism, spirit guides, splitting the atom or light and love, I think we can all agree that contemplating meaning is an essential part of being human. And the meaning we find shapes our choices. It motivates us. It provides us with a kind of framework of understanding, and this framework guides us as we move through life. The framework you align with matters greatly. It can be empowered atheism that appreciates nature and human connection. It can be Judaism, Christianity, Hinduism, Buddhism. It can be a combination of as many different ideas and faiths as you want. It can be atheism meets paganism meets Star Wars. All that matters is that we allow our mind and heart to explore the bigger questions, so we can develop a spiritual framework that facilitates our life. Questions like: What is the meaning of life? What is God? What is wisdom, and how do we connect to it? What is love, and how do we connect to it? What is peace, and how do we connect to it? Are we connected to the people around us, and if so, how?

If you haven't asked yourself these kinds of questions, or if your framework for understanding life is full of fear and hate, I would urge you to explore your own spirituality and find a framework that works *for* you instead of *against* you.

Great relationships

People need respectful, loving relationships to thrive. All people need this, but it's particularly important if you're trying to rebuild after grief, pain, loss or trauma. So far in the book I haven't said much about my research. Here, though, I want to mention it because it takes this idea to another level. It explains it in a way that I think is particularly powerful as we think about how to grow and thrive after trauma.

In a nutshell, *social cure* research has demonstrated that the relationships we have with social groups – from family, to friends, sports groups, work colleagues and more – affects our health, both positively and negatively. The more we *identify* with a group (i.e. the more important it is to us), the more influence the group will have on us. So, if we really identify with a group that perpetuates unhealthy behavioural, cognitive and emotional norms (i.e. alcohol misuse, hostile communication, not talking about feelings) we'd be hard pushed not to adopt the same identity. Of course, if this is working against our deeper values and sense of self, it's going to negatively affect our self-esteem too. The reverse is shown to be true as well. The more we identify with healthy, functional groups, the higher our wellbeing and mental health. We feel good about ourselves because we're part of a group that feels good to us, and helps us be the best version of ourselves. The type of group doesn't matter. It could be a friendship group, our family, the people we work with, college friends, our sports team, a 12-step fellowship, a support group, an online community (whatever). All that matters is that it feels good and reflects the type of identity we want and need.

The take-home from a whole heap of research is that being part of a group isn't just about having a nice time with other people. It's about our identity, our self-concept and our self-esteem. If we want to grow, we need to think carefully about who we spend time with. We need to think about all our relationships, all the groups we're part of, and ask ourselves if these relationships reflect the future we want. Because we have a choice. We can see people less. We can do things on our own terms. We can establish new boundaries. We can change and see if they change with us. We can have honest conversations. We can leave altogether, if we want.

Many people who experience trauma have low self-esteem. We cannot afford to be around people who lower it further. We cannot afford to be around people who drag us back and pull us down. We need to find ways to build our confidence and sense of self. Taking part in relationships that reflect the future we want will help us do this.

Resilience

Life is full of stress. The older I get, the truer I realise this is. There is no point having an expectation that life will one day be a glowing utopia of endless fun and sunshine. The expectation itself will cause me pain because it will never be realised. Life can – and does – include joy and laughter. It includes beautiful moments of connection and a sense of fulfilment. It includes growth and learning. But it's also difficult at times. I don't know what your experience is, but for me, there's *always something*. A child stressed and upset, a problem with work, an issue in my extended family, a work deadline, a house move, a bereavement, a loss. This is life. When I don't accept this fact, I suffer. When I accept it, I see a way through.

My friend called me the other day. Over the sound of her young children screaming and demanding dinner she shouted: 'I'm absolutely certain that this is The Bad Place. Surely, surely, I did something wrong in a past life, and I'm in hell?!'

My friend has a really dry sense of humour. (If you haven't seen the Netflix program *The Good Place* by the way, you should watch it. It's clever and funny, a bit like my friend.) My point is, even when things are *good*, life can be a challenging juggle of priorities, commitments and feelings. If, on top of the *challenging juggle* there's also a *bad* situation, it can be very hard to cope. And if, on top of all of that, you're also trying to manage your trauma and your healing, life can be very painful. It can – and sometimes does – feel like we're living in The Bad Place.

Enter stage left: resilience. Resilience is defined as a person's ability to recover quickly from difficulties. It's about standing back up after you've been knocked down. It's about coping. It's about finding ways to move through adversity, pain and, yes, trauma, and come out the other side. We all need to find healthy ways to cope so it feels less like we're living in The Bad Place. So, no matter how loudly the kids are screaming, or how many things *go wrong*, you can stay sane, connect with your unbreakable core, connect with your strength and know you will be okay.

There's a lot of practical information about what resilience is, and how to increase it. Interestingly, the overarching message is that we can best increase our resilience by taking part in supportive relationships. Another tick in the box for finding our tribe. As well as this, it's about avoiding seeing crises as insurmountable and keeping things in perspective, developing a positive outlook, setting goals and moving towards them, managing our feelings in a healthy way and self-care.[3] Quite the to-do list there! Hop to it, then!

I think about resilience a lot. I practice techniques, try things out and see what works in different situations. I figure out what helps me cope with stress, day by day, minute by minute, in a way that feels good and empowers me, but that doesn't require toxic positivity or pretending. Because resilience *is* being in uncomfortable feelings and situations, without running away, avoiding or pretending. Resilience is honesty; asking for help. It's crying when we need to, self-care, taking time to connect with our core and our adult self. It's leaning on our spiritual beliefs and faith. It's searching for comfort in a power greater than ourselves, whether this is God, nature, love, energy, etc. Resilience isn't powering on through and pretending we're okay; it's stopping and looking after ourselves. Sometimes resilience is calling a friend and making a joke about the fact we're all living in The Bad Place.

What's all this growth mindset jargon?

Maybe this chapter is feeling a little heavy on the terminology, but just one more: growth mindset. It's used a lot nowadays by life and business coaches, but behind the 'grow your business' message is a beautiful sentiment and solid research. It started with Dr Carol Dweck, a professor of psychology at Stanford University, who studied seventh-grade children's attitudes towards failure and intelligence. It became clear that children did better at school if they had a growth mindset – if they believed they could get smarter and understood that effort made them stronger. Later research demonstrated that it's possible to move children from a fixed mindset (believing that our intelligence and talents are fixed traits and cannot be changed) to a growth mindset. Backing up all this lovely solution-focused research are the neuroscientific discoveries into neural plasticity, which I mentioned in chapter five (p. 134). This awesome research demonstrates our innate ability to learn, change and grow.[4] No unicorns, but nice, fluffy, positive stuff.

I mention this to point out to you that, as you're considering change and new possibilities, you have a choice. You can adopt a fixed mindset (*I can't learn or change and my efforts won't make any difference*), or you can try to implement a growth mindset (*I can learn and change, and my efforts will make a difference*). I'll admit that it sounds a bit jargon-y, but I think we should all get over it and hop on board. I've only recently discovered the growth mindset research, but it fits with so much of what I've observed, and personally practised, over the past fifteen years.

Have you noticed that very few people talk about how resilience and the growth mindset relate to trauma healing? People presume this stuff – that's all about strength and thriving – isn't relevant in this space. Well, it absolutely is relevant here.

I want to tell you about Mila. Mila's mother had severe anorexia and passed away when she was about six years old. Her father had always been distant and distracted, but once her mother passed away it felt like he barely engaged with her at all. When Mila was eight, her father remarried a much younger woman whom Mila resented and hated to be around. Mila played up at school and at home. She was rude, defiant and often in trouble. After she was caught smoking at the tender age of ten, Mila was sent off to boarding school, where she stayed until she was eighteen. She visited

home once a month and, over time, her family relationships became easier. However, she did, over the same time,
develop bulimia. And, as is the case with so many young
teens, she also discovered alcohol. The drinking and the
bulimia allowed her to cope with her buried trauma, her
pain, her grief and her loss.

Mila's father eventually cottoned on to the fact that his
daughter was spiralling out of control, and she was sent to a
rehab centre when she was twenty-one. Scan forward three
years and Mila is living in London attempting to piece her
life back together. She no longer drinks, has a big support
network and sees a therapist every week. She's happier and
feels more connected to herself, but life is still hard. Mila
has a job at a women's clothing store. Showing up daily is
hard because now that she's not numbing her feelings, she
has a lot of them. But her commitment is helping rebuild
her self-esteem, so she knows *showing up* is the best thing.

Fast forward two more years and Mila is increasingly
strong and confident. She's always wanted to set up her own
online shop so she buys the domain name and some stock
and runs the business in the evening after she's finished her
day job in the store. It's hard and there are a lot of things to
learn along the way. After six months of stress and effort,
it's clear the online shop isn't working. She's tried a lot of
different ways to make it fly, but it's losing money. Accepting
this is painful, but she does accept it. She closes the online
business and has a very difficult few months as the failure
and loss of the shop trigger her trauma and her grief.

So, you're likely wondering where I'm going with this

story. Surely that can't be the end of the tale? Not in a chapter about resilience and growth! It's not, but I have to say that even if this was the end of the tale, I'd say that Mila has demonstrated amazing resilience, determination and commitment. She's epitomised a growth mindset because she's let herself grow, learn, fail, get back up, grow a bit more, fail again, and try again. She's a warrior.

After a difficult few months, during which Mila worked through her triggered trauma and leaned heavily on those around her for support, she started another online business. I feel emotional as I remember the conversation we had about six months after she'd relaunched her business. She bounded into the coffee shop, all energised and glowing.

'Hello you,' I said with a smile. 'You look so happy.'

'I really am,' Mila beamed. 'The business is doing so great.'

Mila proceeded to tell me how her business was doing so well that she had been able to drop down to part-time at her job in the store. She'd rebranded and started marketing in a different way, and it had made a big difference. She said how dificult it was sometimes, and how she had to work hard to keep her self-esteem from 'bottoming out'. This, she said, was the main challenge. The business was hard work, but managing the 'mean girl' in her head was the main task. She was learning to ride out and control the eruptions of negative thinking, triggered beliefs, anxiety and fear. She was allowing herself to learn and make mistakes. She understood that the effort it took to stand back up after being knocked down demonstrated huge strength. She was developing a meaningful resilience that enabled her to thrive.

Mila has been a big source of inspiration for me over the years. I'm grateful to her and all the other warriors I've met along the way. People who keep trying, keep growing and keep believing that freedom and success are possible. People who face their past and take responsibility for their lives today. Men and women who get honest and real (even though it hurts), and courageously break their negative life patterns. People who demonstrate that thriving after trauma, addiction, pain, grief and loss is very possible indeed.

Success

When I ask people what success means to them, most say something about having a great, fulfilling job and earning a good salary. Sometimes people mention success being linked to happiness or falling in love. That pretty much sums it up – good job, lots of money, happiness, gooey love. Not bad goals, that's for sure. But, to me, those goals feel a little bit Hollywood. They're the goals of the movies; the goals we're told to want. Other than happiness – which, I might add, is a very elusive goal – the other aspects of success are external to us. Money. Job. Relationship. These are important, but they're all about who we are in the world, not who we are at our core.

As I've grown, as I have done my work, success is now more personal to me. For me, success means putting myself out there, even if I might fail. It means being present and grounded. It means listening, observing and acting – not reacting. It means deepening my connection with my unbreakable core, God and the divine, and with my instincts, love and wisdom. It means deepening my connection with the people I love. It means learning to be the mother that my children want and need. Success means being willing to keep learning and growing. It means reaching for joy and laughter, always, because otherwise what are we doing here? For me, it means having a fulfilling career and earning a good salary, yes, but not at the expense of my mental and spiritual health. Success for me is about moving forward in a balanced, connected, grounded, honest way.

Before you move on to the next chapter, I'd encourage you to think about what success means for you. Your answer to this question is important, because this book isn't just about seeing how the past is preventing you from moving forward, it's also about actually moving forward. First, we step out of the loop, then we flow into the future we want. The specifics of what you want might change as you grow, but the answer to this question – what does success mean to you? – is, in my experience, unlikely to change.

I need to add a little cautionary note about how your traumatic beliefs will react at the idea of your success. They're going to make this puking, scoffing, guffawing noise. They're going to try to ruin this for you. Just like they did when you were paid that compliment, or offered the promotion, or thought about setting up a business. I'm just giving you a heads up. My experience has taught me that as I take a step forward my old beliefs react. They get pretty pissed off. They tell me to get back in my box. Sometimes I can see them and laugh at them. Sometimes I have to calm and soothe them. Sometimes I have to tell them to *fuck off*. I'd highly recommend you adopt the same strategy if you feel their stifling presence as you try to contemplate the idea of your own success. I'm certain that it's time for you to say *enough*, and step into your own version of success.

Chapter Eight

The tools

This chapter gives you some practical tools to use to shift out of old traumatic life patterns and loops. They're methods and techniques that I've been taught by incredible practitioners and then adapted or developed myself, over the years. Many are tools that I still use daily.

The tools are designed to help you break the Trauma Loop. They're a gentle balance of somatic (body), cognitive (mind) and behavioural tools to help you break free from patterns you might be stuck in. As you break free, you'll reconnect to your feelings, your body, your core and your highest adult self. This is how we heal our trauma in this book: we heal how it shows up in our life today. We break patterns, we let our feelings flow, we reconnect, we shift from old to new.

You might not succeed right away, and that's glorious. Let these tools feel new and uncomfortable. Let yourself have a bad day. Let yourself take a break. Then stand back up and try again. Don't give up. That's resilience. That's how you *become* stronger. Let yourself learn. The outcomes – freedom, strength and purpose – are worth it.

Notes on how to use these tools

1. These are tools to dip in and out of, not a structured program. Choose the tool that resonates with you the most, and practise. Play around with it, see if it's a good fit for you. Don't try to start all of the tools at once – you'll be setting yourself up to burn out and give up. Maybe you'll end up using all ten tools, maybe you'll use two or three. If *all* you take from this chapter is one rock-solid tool, that's great, too. That's enough; that's growth and healing. Take what you want and leave the rest.

2. Be guided by your body and your sense of safety. Each tool should feel like a challenge, but none of them should feel overwhelming or unsafe. If any of the tools make your symptoms and reactions worse, stop. What I dearly want is for you to connect to your core and your instincts. And if, as you work with your body, your instinct guides you away from a tool, trust your instinct implicitly. You know what is best for you.

3. Meaningful personal growth and healing is something we do over years and years. It doesn't end. I'm still doing it, and so is the most Zen eighty-year-old you know. It's a journey that involves soft, gentle growth alongside some hard, painful growth. Sometimes there's a fundamental

shift, like for me at the ashram. More often it's about putting in the footwork, and making daily changes that add up over time to a big shift. You can't rush it and anyone who tells you there's a quick fix doesn't fully understand the nature of trauma. Slow and steady works. Yes, there might be a leap, a transformative moment, but it only counts if you build on it. Make changes that can last. Create something solid. Transformation is possible, but only if you put in the work over time. Healing is about replacing reactions with actions. We step into considered, moderate, thoughtful actions. Of course, this cannot be rushed.

4. Before we move forward, I need to be very clear that these tools are for people who carry trauma and who experience triggered traumatic sensations, feelings, thoughts or behaviours in their lives today. But they are not appropriate if you are extremely unwell and unable to function because of your trauma. If this is you, please find professional face-to-face support.

5. Likewise, if you're already working with a therapist or undertaking trauma work, please consider how appropriate it is to use these tools alongside your current therapeutic process. Discuss them with your therapist. Consider how useful the tools will be in the context of other work you're doing.

6. Do you remember in chapter one I mentioned that we can only feel our feelings when we feel safe? This is something to remember as you use these tools. The safer we feel, the more likely it is that our trapped emotions, which

relate to our trauma, are going to surface. As we stabilise and reconnect, our subconscious does wonderful things. It thinks: okay, she's ready now, we can let her feel.

As well as this, be aware that when we break out of a cycle or pattern, we often feel all the feelings we were trying to avoid. Moving out of a deeply ingrained pattern can bring up feelings of grief, anger, fear or loss. This is normal: allow your feelings to flow as you make the changes you need to. Some of these tools are designed to help you process feelings that come up. Tool five helps you feel and release, tool seven encourages you to find support on your journey. If you feel overwhelmed by any feelings, thoughts or memories that come up as you use the tools, please immediately seek professional support.

7. A final note. Any changes that you undertake in life require effort. They can be tiring. You might find it easy-breezy to implement these tools, but it's more likely that they'll feel like a stretch emotionally, cognitively and physically. That's good, that's the growth. A stretch – an effort – is what we're looking for (painful pushing is not, though). This effort requires energy, so do yourself a favour and look after yourself. Get to bed on time. Eat right. Find support. You know, the stuff Mary Poppins would tell you to do. Try, at least try, to look after your lovely self as you test out some of these tools in your life.

Tool one – setting your intentions and your path

This tool is part practical and part spiritual, with a bit of woo-woo law of attraction thrown in. (For those who haven't heard of the *law of attraction*, I'm referring to the principle that what we focus on and think about creates our reality.) So, you're going to build a clear vision for yourself and set some intentions. All the tools help us shift out of old reactions and patterns. But as you let go of the old, what are you going to step into? Without an idea of what we're seeking, letting go of the old can feel overwhelming. It's easy to end up feeling out of control. A vision of the future provides us with much needed direction and structure. It holds us in a way that is hard to explain but feels very powerful. So don't underestimate this tool!

Take your time as you answer the following questions. To be clear, this tool isn't *about* trauma. Your vision doesn't have to incorporate any of the themes you've read about in the book (although for many people it does). This is the big ticket, blue-sky thinking part of the tools. It's about learning more about what you want, connecting to your core and constructing a strong adult self and identity. Try to enjoy it, and don't hold back. Don't overthink these questions – allow your feelings and your heart to lead, not your head. Before you start, take a few deep slow breaths and focus on your heart centre. Allow yourself to find stillness, and connection with the body.

- What are you seeking in your relationships?
- What are you seeking in your health and wellbeing?
- What are you seeking in your work?
- When you picture your life a year from now, what do you want it to look like?

The first three questions help us see – and set – our intentions. From your answers about what you're seeking, you'll be able to define some clear intentions for yourself to use in different situations or on different days. For example, I am seeking deeper emotional connection in my close relationships . . . so my intention is to be more honest and open about how I'm feeling. To support your intentions you can also create affirmations to use throughout the day. For example, affirmations like *I'm deeply connected to those I love* or *it's safe to be open about my feelings* or *I state my feelings honestly* would support this particular intention. You can say them out loud, in your mind as a mantra, or write them down and stick them where you can see them.

I use intentions often, but especially if I feel it's time to make a change. When we set them, we give ourselves a clear guide to come back to throughout the day. If we set an intention in the morning and over the course of the day we realise our actions are not aligned with the intention, we're usually able to clearly see what's thrown us off course. Usually the things that throw us off and pull us away from our intentions relate to our trauma-led patterns (e.g. being triggered into shame and therefore feeling unable to be honest and open with people). This is the gold: information about our triggers, and what we need to heal.

Your answer to the last question will draw from the previous three. It's about hopes, dreams and desires. When you ask yourself what you want, what do you see? What do you want your life to look like a year from now? Don't write down what it *should* look like, write down what you *want* it to look like.

You know one of the worst things about trauma? It keeps us focused on the past, so our future ends up being a carbon copy of what happened before. To change, we gently remind ourselves to refocus on what we want. So, what do you want?

Tool two – daily practice

This tool is about reconnecting with our core and our body in a new way. It combines visualisations with somatic theories and practices. It enables us to visualise health and strength, and also learn to focus on the central parts of our body. This kind of *new* embodiment is critical in trauma healing.

Achieving change, personal growth and healing over the long term requires putting one foot in front of the other each day. The notion of daily commitment in the form of a daily practice sits at the heart of this. As well as being about reconnection and embodiment, this tool is also about taking personal responsibility and showing up for ourselves on a daily basis.

Every day I recommit to a decision that I made all those years ago, when I committed to healing. What this means, in the context of my life, is that I make a daily commitment to live in *recovery*, not in my trauma. I love the term *recovery*, but I know some people find the word hard to relate to. It can sound too extreme, too medical, too addiction-y. If the word *recovery* really grates, pick a different one. It's the meaning that matters, not the word. Perhaps you will commit to *growth*. Perhaps you will commit to *change*. Perhaps you will commit to *healing*. Perhaps you will commit to *honesty*, or maybe to *love*. Whichever words you chose, whichever word resonates with you, it's the meaning that matters. The meaning behind my daily commitment, and yours, goes something like this:

- It's a commitment to breaking old patterns and stepping into a new way of being.
- It's a commitment to honest self-observation.
- It's a commitment to finding our core and connecting to our true self.
- It's a commitment to taking responsibility for our own feelings, behaviours and thoughts today, no matter what happened in the past.
- Ultimately, it's a commitment to the process of growing and learning.

This is the daily commitment, which you'll wrap up in a daily practice because daily rituals (i.e. habits and routines) are the key to long-term change. You don't have to use the exact ritual I've outlined on the next page, but you need something strong and powerful. It must be reverent. It must help you connect to your body and your *core*. It must help you ground.

Most often, for my daily ritual I sit cross-legged, eyes closed, spine strong and tall, in my meditation corner. I sit on the same orange meditation cushion that I used at the ashram, and I have my beautiful crystals around me. If it's a busy get-the-kids-to-school morning, I take five minutes. If I've got more time, I sit for longer.

Like me, many people have a certain place in their home they like to use for their daily ritual (e.g. a meditation space, or somewhere soulful and meaningful). Some people like to use objects (e.g. candles, crystals, a singing bowl, sage or a specific pillow to sit on). Some create an altar. The reverence matters because *you* matter. It's about respect and honour, for yourself and the changes you're being brave enough to make. If you're used to taking the piss out of life, this reverence is going to feel icky and laughable. I highly recommend you put down the defensive sarcasm (I can relate by the way), light a candle and give it a whirl. Stretch yourself. Grow.

Every morning, before you get on with the day, take some time to connect and remind your mind and body of the commitment you're making today. Consistency matters, as this creates the structure and routine that becomes a powerful cue to your new way of being. Whether you live in the mountains in Arizona or a tower block in London, Sydney or New York, it's possible to create reverence and connection. So, find a space within your home that feels peaceful. Create a sense of reverence within it – show the process, and yourself, some respect. Use the ritual below or adapt it to create something personal to you.

Suggested daily practice

1. Sit on a cushion on the floor, or on a chair. The position must feel strong, not slouchy, but should be comfortable. Close your eyes *(optional)*.
2. Take some deep, slow breaths into your belly (in for four, out for eight), then breathe normally. With each exhale, let go of tension – really arrive in the moment, into your practice and your body.
3. When you're ready, focus on the gentle movement of your breath in your chest and heart space. Notice how the ribs expand in every direction. Breathe here for as long as you wish.
4. When you're ready, focus on the centre of your heart space and visualise a bright light here. Perhaps it pulses as you breathe, white light filling your entire chest space as you inhale. Perhaps the light expands into your belly and through your shoulders into the top of your arms if the inhale is deep. Play with it; notice it change as your body and breath change and respond to it. Perhaps the light travels all the way to the crown of your head, your feet, or somewhere else that needs healing and strength. Or perhaps comfort comes from being still with this central light, your breath so calm, so gentle, so slow, that your chest barely moves and the light is beautifully still. *Stay with this loving light for as long as you need.*
5. When you're ready, focus again on the centre of your heart space – the central light, where it shines strong and bright and deep. Say to yourself:
    I connect to *my unbreakable core;**
    I commit to honesty and daily action;
    and I open to love, healing and wisdom.
6. Say it once or twice, or repeat (all of it, or some of it) as a mantra while you focus on the light or the centre of your heart space.
7. As you practise connecting with your heart centre, your

mind is likely to wander. Gently bring your attention back if/when it does. Even If you can remain here for just a few seconds, that's enough.

8. When you're ready to leave this space, take a few deep, slow breaths into your belly. Return your awareness to your physical body – perhaps wiggle your toes or stretch your arms. Bow your head, thank your body for its strength and healing, and then gently open your eyes.

9. If you need to, stay in this space longer. Take the time you need to connect to yourself.

* Please personalise this – use a term that feels comfortable and natural for you, and change it as often as you need. *Unbroken core*, *love*, *healing energy*, *God*, *strength*, *soul*, *peace* or *wholeness* are some examples. Go with what feels right for you.

You must connect with this ritual – you must mean it and feel into it – but it can take anywhere between 2 and 20 minutes. If you have time and it feels good, sit for longer with the meditations and the mantras; take the time you need. If you have to get on with the day, do the ritual concisely. Practise daily – strengthen your connection to your breath, your body and your centre. Repeat this practice during the day if you want to or need to. Return to the calm, loving, wisdom of your heart space, or the healing light, as often as you need.

Tool three – joining the dots

People often contact me saying they want to do their trauma work, but they don't know where to start. *Trauma work* involves understanding, releasing or processing our past trauma to stop it negatively affecting life today. And there are many, many ways we can do this work. Some deep trauma work requires us to process our past experiences with a therapist or psychologist. The trauma work we're doing here isn't about looking back, it's about looking to today. Tool three, if carried out with honesty and with rigour, is a type of *trauma work*. It's designed to help us understand the Trauma Loops that we're stuck in, and if combined with the other tools, can help us break free from our past.

This tool is about observing your daily life, yourself, your reactions, physical sensations, feelings, thoughts and behaviour. In doing so, you will establish:

1. What triggers you.
2. What your triggered reaction is (i.e. what you experience, feel, think, believe and do to cope or avoid the reaction).
3. Which past experience the trigger and reaction stem from (*optional*).

The first step is easy: buy a notebook and find a pen. The second is less easy: honesty and courage. This exercise requires us to be honest about what we're experiencing and to courageously notice (and therefore be with) our uncomfortable reactions and feelings. If you're not ready today, come back to this tool at a later date.

I know it's tempting to observe yourself without writing

things down, but keeping a journal over time allows us to see our patterns and Trauma Loops. You can organise the notebook any way you like. A simple method is to use it as a daily diary that you write in at the end of the day. Or, if it helps, write down details during the day as you become aware of a specific trigger or triggered reaction. Make a note of today's date at the top of the page, then make a note of roughly what you did during the day (e.g. *ran late in the morning, worked, quick lunch, saw Mum after work*). It's also worth noting down anything specific about how you were feeling or what was going on internally (e.g. *bad night's sleep, woke up feeling anxious*). Then, answer the two (or three) questions. Some days, nothing will trigger you. This is useful to know too. Below is an example of the work.

Over time, you'll build up a picture of who or what triggers you and when, or how.

You'll be able to see your Trauma Loops: the trigger and the triggered cascade of reactions in your body, mind and behaviour. Don't be a perfectionist about finding your trauma loops, though. Sometimes we notice only the triggered physical reaction; other times we clearly observe the reaction in our mind (e.g. our negative thinking and triggered old beliefs) but are unaware of the emotional reaction. You don't need to observe *every* aspect of the Trauma Loop every time you're triggered. Clarity comes over time – it's about noticing what repetitively triggers a reaction and how that reaction often manifests. This is how we see the patterns, and over time observe the loops we're trapped in.

Notes on tool three:

1. Any trigger that provokes a strong reaction in you should be noted down. This could be a conversation, a situation, a smell, a person, a place, feeling – anything. Although not all the things you react to in life are reminders of a past trauma, over time you'll see what's repeated and intense (and therefore more likely to relate to the past).

2. Noticing our physical reactions and sensations and the effect a triggered emotion has on our body is something we learn over time. The more you work with this tool – which, at heart, is about honest observation – the better you'll be able to notice how your body changes when it's triggered.

3. It's usually fairly easy to spot our conscious cognitive reactions (e.g. racing thoughts, negative thinking, going into fantasy, brain fog, etc.), but it's harder to spot our triggered beliefs (e.g. *I'm a failure, I'm bad, people can't be trusted*). This is because until we're aware of them, these beliefs tend to operate subconsciously. This tool is likely to begin to bring these beliefs to consciousness, but still they can be hard to spot. Write down the triggered beliefs if you become aware of them as you do this work, but don't be disheartened if this aspect of the Trauma Loop remains a little foggy. Trust that over time these old beliefs will become clear. Please see page 30 for a list of some common self-limiting beliefs.

4. All behaviours that accompany or follow a strong physical, emotional and/or cognitive reaction to a trigger should be noted down. Some of these will be destructive (they're part of the Trauma Loop). Others will be empowering

(these are not part of the cycle). Note them all down so you can see over time which behaviours help you break the reaction, and which keep you trapped in the loop. Examples of self-limiting or destructive behaviours are on pages 80 to 81.

In Lucy's workbook, it's clear from just three days of observations that avoiding people is one of her primary behavioural responses to being triggered. On Thursday she avoids people at work and leaves early, and on Saturday she cancels seeing her friend, Helen. She also binge-eats in response to a major trigger around her family. We also see one of Lucy's triggered beliefs – that she's a failure – and that this belief is accompanied by triggered feelings of shame and fear. Importantly, we also see that, when she shares her feelings with her most trusted friends, her triggered response from the previous day lessens.

Lucy chooses to think about the past, but if this feels too confronting, please don't do this. It's important that you don't push yourself to remember. If the connection between the trigger/reaction and a past experience is obvious and comes straight to mind, then note it down. But don't search; don't push. That type of work may require someone to be there next to you. If you do choose to think about the past, please trust whatever comes up. Don't overthink it. Don't dismiss what you see, feel or think. So many people, myself included, censor the information their subconscious shows them.

If you do want to consider how your triggered reaction relates to the past, you can do this immediately after you've been triggered or later in the day once you've reconnected

Lucy's workbook

Thursday 13 February

Today: A work day, then went to the gym in the evening, feeling tired but positive.

Trigger: Triggered during an awkward conversation with Mel about a problem at work.

Reaction: I felt really ashamed and fearful and like a total failure. Hard to keep it together. I avoided her and everyone else all day, and left work early.

Past? Feel it might link to Mum, but not sure why I think that.

Friday 14 February

Today: Off work, had a run in the morning with Helen and Rose, met Helen for lunch, mooched around the shops, had an early night. Woke up feeling upset about yesterday, still fearful and anxious but less shame. Spoke with Helen and Rose, and the fear-y feelings shifted.

Not triggered today.

Saturday 15 February

Today: Off work, had a run in the morning, saw my parents for lunch.

Trigger: Triggered by Mum talking about the family.

Reaction: I felt totally out of body and dissociated. No obvious thoughts at the time, just a racing mind and feeling really awful. Had a huge food binge when I got home and cancelled seeing Helen in the evening.

Past? Definitely relates to what happened with my uncle.

to your core. If you wish to do this, take some deep, slow breaths into your belly (in for four, out for eight), then breathe normally and gently begin to focus on your heart space. Then ask yourself: *which past experience does this relate to?* Or *who does my reaction relate to?*

The information Lucy noted down, and the patterns that emerge, is the gold. Knowledge is power. As I've said before, these muddy painful truths are the gateway to meaningful change. Lucy can now choose what to do. She can work with the other tools to decrease, and learn to control, her triggered reactions. She can practise tool two every morning to help strengthen her connection to her core. She can use tool four to reconnect to herself after she's been triggered. She could use tool five to feel her feelings and learn to release them, and use tool six to rein in her negative thinking, or she can help build her resilience and connection to others by using tool seven. By working with the tools, she may be able to break her Trauma Loops. I hope she can, but she may need more help. *You* might need more help. If you can make meaningful, lasting changes on your own, all power to you. But if you need more help, more support, that too is great. For some, these tools are enough. For many others, they're just the start of their trauma work.

Tool four – trigger 'n' ground

This is the simplest and the most powerful tool because it moves you from your past trauma to your present self. It's about spotting and then *owning* your triggered reaction.

By doing so you reclaim your body, your mind and your life – one moment at a time. When we're triggered we're thrown backwards; when we ground we come back to ourselves today, in the present moment.

Grounding and centring needs to replace the cascade of traumatic reactions. It takes practice and a commitment to growth, change and learning (e.g. tool two). Our overwhelm and powerlessness make us believe a lot of things that aren't true. They make us believe we cannot control our minds and our bodies. But in many instances we can interrupt the response and calm the reaction. You *can* ground yourself. You can get your prefrontal cortex – the planning, decision-making and self-control part of our brain, remember – working again. You can reconnect to your core and your adult self today.

This tool has two parts. The first involves realising that you're triggered and owning your reaction. The second is pulling back from it.

1. Say (out loud or in your mind): I am triggered so (name the physical, emotional, cognitive or behavioural reaction). For example:
   - I am triggered so I feel overwhelmed.
   - I am triggered so I feel ashamed.
   - I am triggered so I've dissociated.
   - I am triggered so my heart is racing.
   - I am triggered so I think I'm a failure.
   - I am triggered so I think everyone is out to get me.
   - I am triggered so I want to binge-eat.
2. Take slow deep breaths (in for four, out for eight).

3. GROUND, GROUND, GROUND: use the safety and reconnection grounding techniques described in chapter three.
4. Use the discharging energy techniques if you need to (i.e. if you're still experiencing fight or flight symptoms such as anxiety, racing heart, etc.). Please note that you should first make yourself feel safe and reconnect to the present moment, *then* you release the trapped fight or flight energy if you need to. Not everyone needs this kind of energetic release. For many it's enough to feel safe and reconnect to themselves.[1]

See pages 41 and 42 for a full list of grounding and discharging energy techniques and an explanation of why we use them. Tool up, test them out and figure out which works best in different situations. Some days one technique is enough. Other days, we might need to use many of the techniques and take our time. Let yourself learn, let yourself fail, stand up and try again.

It's likely that there are going to be times when you can't ground and reconnect to your self today, no matter how much you've practised or how committed you are to healing. If the triggered reaction is strong, grounding and reconnecting can feel impossible. Over time it's likely that this will change. In the interim, if we cannot provide ourselves with a sense of solid, grounded safety we find another person who can. We reach out for help. We cuddle someone, look into someone's eyes or talk to someone who can help us co-regulate. Open up to your partner or to a close friend. Make a call. Find meaningful support. Find your people (see tool seven).

Tool five – feel your feelings

This tool, and what it represents, is my nemesis. For that reason, it has also brought me the greatest healing. I just didn't *get* this whole 'feel your feelings' thing. I couldn't get it because I was disconnected from my body (which is where we feel our feelings) and therefore, my core, my wisdom and my instincts. I had to do gentle body work with a therapist to reconnect to my body and my emotions. Even with help, it took me a really long time to make progress. The honest truth is that I don't know if I could have practised this reconnection at home. This book wasn't available to me when I was *in it*, so I'll never know, but I suspect that it would have been too overwhelming and confronting. So why have I included it? Because firstly, though it's my nemesis, it may not be yours and secondly, even if it is, it's better that you know.

In chapter five I gave a very brief introduction to the fact that feelings are experienced in the body. We don't *think* a feeling, we *feel* it. Where? In our body. Some of you are thinking, 'Errrr, duh, obviously,' (this definitely isn't your nemesis), whereas others might be 'Errrr, I hear you, but what?' (sorry, but this might be your nemesis). One of the reasons body work and somatic psychotherapy are so critically important within trauma work is because they teach us how to be in our body and experience our emotions from within it. The body holds so much information: so many feelings, so many memories. Trauma disconnects us. Body work gently reconnects us.

This reconnection can be extremely hard, uncomfortable

or even frightening, if you carry considerable trauma. Please be aware of this as you decide whether to use this tool. If it doesn't feel right, if it feels too confronting, overwhelming or confusing, save this kind of work for another day.

There are two versions of this tool. One is a body-work exercise to use at home; the other is to incorporate into your daily life.

This is the tool that carries the strongest warning, because although I want you to strengthen your connection to your body, I don't want to unlock feelings, memories, sensations or trauma that feel *too much* today as you work on this at home. So, as with all the tools, feel your way through this exercise and use it wisely. If this gets too much (e.g. you feel overwhelmed, frightened, unsafe) stop immediately. If, when you come into your body, you're confronted by memories you aren't ready for or do not want to engage with, stop immediately. I felt this way many times. It doesn't signal dysfunction. It doesn't mean you're broken or damaged. It doesn't mean you're not strong enough to *go there*. All it tells you is that you need a greater sense of safety (such as being supported by a therapist, or being further into your healing) as you access some of your feelings. Listen to your body – it knows best.

The second version of this exercise, on the next page, helps you incorporate this body work into your daily life. This is also less confronting than the previous version, so it's a good one to use if the first part of the tool was too overwhelming. This version of the tool helps us begin to physically locate emotions (good or bad) that we experience during the day.

At-home exercise

1. Close your eyes (optional). Take deep slow polyvagal breaths into your belly (e.g. in for four, out for eight), then breathe normally.

2. When you're ready, focus on your stomach and gently breathe.

3. As you remain focused on your stomach, ask yourself: *how do you feel?*

4. Observe what comes up. Perhaps you hear your answer in your mind, perhaps you sense it in your gut. Perhaps it's unclear. That's very common. You may get clearer about how you feel as you move through the exercise.

5. Name the feeling(s) if you can (e.g. *I feel sad*).

6. Notice and describe any physical sensations (e.g. *I have a lump in my throat, a solid feeling in my chest and a pressure around my eyes*).

7. Come back to the stomach. Breathe, observe.

8. Notice if anything else comes up. Do any images come to mind? Do you hear or see any words? Be curious. Notice what you see, hear and feel. Dismiss nothing.

9. If it feels okay, ask your body: *what do you need?* (e.g. *I need to cry, I need to be held*). If it feels safe to do so, give your body what it needs.

10. When you're ready, bring your attention back to your heart space, focusing on this central point to reconnect to your core. Breathe, take your time. When you're ready, gently open your eyes.

It's simple, but it's also powerful. It strengthens our mind–body connection, helps us reconnect to our true feelings, and helps us move out of trauma-led cycles we might be stuck in.

Not all emotions are part of a triggered traumatic reaction – far from it. Emotions are normal, healthy, sensual, beautiful aspects of being human. Our emotions are there to guide us. Moving towards them, as both versions of this tool encourage, is an eye-opening journey if we're not used to being with our feelings (let alone our body). Owning our feelings is an essential part of growth and resilience. We must notice them, allow them and love them. We need to observe them and trust they will pass (which they always do, whether they're part of a triggered reaction or not).

Daily life exercise
1. Notice, then name any emotion (big or small) as it's happening, while you go about your daily life. For example, perhaps you're at work and notice that you're beginning to feel angry. Pause and say to yourself, 'I'm feeling angry.'
2. Now, gently observe where and how you experience this emotion in your body. How do you know you're angry? Where do you feel it? What type of sensation is it? (e.g. *I'm feeling angry, my jaw is clenched and tense, my chest feels tight and compressed, I have a feeling of pressure around my eyes and in my head*).

Please note that as well as feeling our feelings, finding healthy ways to discharge emotions when they're pent up and stuck is critical. Here are a few:

- *Speaking* them is one of the best ways. Talk to someone, or to yourself, or to God (if that's your thing).
- *Writing* them (e.g. in your journal).
- *Moving* them (i.e. shift your body and your energy). Listen to the body and do what it needs (punch a cushion or the air, stamp your feet, cry without holding back, shout, run on the spot, dance, hug yourself). Don't hold back. Help your body discharge the pent-up feelings and energy when it needs to.
- *Letting go* of them (e.g. letting go of the emotional tension by letting go of the physical tension). Using the 'Daily life exercise' as an example, this would mean relaxing the jaw, using the breath to release the chest, and consciously relaxing the muscles around the eyes.

It's worth mentioning that anxiety and anger often mask other feelings. So, although these extreme physical emotions seem easy to recognise, be aware that there may be something else underneath. Fear, shame and sadness are often at their root. If anxiety or anger consistently comes up for you, begin to get curious about what else might be there. I felt anxiety – literally, only anxiety – for about a decade. I rarely feel anxiety today. Instead, I now feel the full spectrum of feelings. Be aware that feeling *stuck* in an emotion is a common trauma symptom, so if you cannot access other feelings (as I couldn't) you may need to find more support.

Tool six – rein in the mind

Negative thinking and negative self-beliefs are the bane of my own, and most other people's, existence. As I've explained in the book, some of these types of cognitions are born from past traumatic experiences. Finding a way out of the old loops that we're stuck in always involves reining in the mind. As we take back control of our thinking, we have better control over our body and behaviour. We say *enough*. This is part of our daily commitment – a commitment to break old cycles, break negative thought patterns and question our self-limiting traumatic beliefs.

Negative thinking is habitual and tends to spiral (meaning things get worse and worse in there). It can feel as if you're fighting a war with yourself – that your mind (your thinking) wants you to lie down and give up. That ashamed, angry, brutal, hateful voice *is* your trauma. It's the part of you that was hurt: the younger you, the frightened you. It needs to be loved, but unfortunately we tend to respond to this voice with cruelty. No good comes from this. The cruelty just fuels the fear and the shame. Calm reassurance, love, gentleness, patience, structure, strength, faith and hope. These are the things that will heal this voice in that difficult moment when you need it to be silenced, and more permanently in the long-term. Speak to this voice as if it's a child. Sometimes this voice needs you to be strong (*no, enough*), other times it needs you to be gentle (*you're frightened, that's okay*), but it is critical that you learn never to respond cruelly.

I've covered loads of specific negative cognitions and beliefs in the book already, so I won't repeat myself. But please see pages 30 and 146 to 147 for an overview. Cognitively, as well as those dangerous and damaging cognitions, the shame and fear push us into common traumatic thinking patterns:

- Mind-reading (guessing, second guessing, guessing again what others are thinking)
- Shoulds (*I should be working harder*)
- Self-sabotaging (*what's the point in trying, I might as well give up*)
- Destructive decision-making (*I'm going to give up*)
- Worry and rumination (running over and over the same thing in your mind)
- Black-and-white thinking (*I'm right, you're wrong* – not being able to find a measured middle-ground)
- Catastrophising (*I'm definitely going to lose my job because I made that little mistake*).

Instead of listening, watching and observing with interest, our thoughts erupt. We're triggered into judgement, negativity and fear. The thinking is a reaction to a perceived threat, so it's always a manifestation of fear. But we're unable to see this, so we take the thoughts to mean something concrete and absolute. We believe our triggered, self-destructive conclusions, when we should give them a cuddle and put them to bed.

There are many ways to combat repetitive, triggered, out of control, fear-led negative thinking. They all involve observing your negative thinking to allow you to separate from it. Often these techniques involve fact-checking whether the thoughts have any basis in reality. Many techniques also involve connecting to the body, whether that's through mindfulness, meditation, the breath or visualisations.

This tool draws on, and combines, these common techniques. I've included naming and owning your feelings, which is something we should all be doing as much as possible. It also includes positive affirmations, because I don't believe we can permanently shift from *the negative* unless we practise *the positive*. There are five steps to this tool:

1. Notice your negative thinking (e.g. *I'm worrying that the house sale will fall through*) and your emotional and physical feelings (*I'm feeling out of control and fearful, my chest is tight, my breathing is shallow and my hands feel tingly*).
2. Fact-check (*Yes, sometimes house sales fall through, but today it's all going through without an issue*).
3. Reconnect to the body and the breath. Take deep, very slow, breaths down into your belly, focusing on the expansion and contraction of the stomach, following the 4/8 rule.
4. Reconnect to your core. Once your body feels calmer, picture a light in the centre of your chest, or focus on

your heart centre. Focus on your core, while gently breathing, for as long as you need.

5. Find an affirmation that feels like it counters the negative belief or thought (e.g. *Everything in life is exactly as it should be*), and repeat mentally or out loud as often as you need during the day.

I use this tool frequently. Usually, once I've followed the five steps and found an affirmation that works for me, repeating the affirmation is enough to move out of (and stay out of) negative thinking. But sometimes, if I'm really *in fear*, I have to repeat the steps many times a day.

Some days this tool can feel extremely difficult because if we're really *in it,* our negative, hurt younger self is going to shout this at us: 'WHAT'S THE POINT? GIVE UP, THIS WON'T WORK.' But we do it anyway, despite the pushback. Our traumatised old self doesn't want us to change. It thinks staying on high alert and being ready to pounce (i.e. staying in our traumatic reaction) is what we need. But it's wrong. We can acknowledge its fear, negativity and judgement, and then carry on because we've committed to daily action.

The loop of negative thinking doesn't end, unless we intervene with love. So we take responsibility for our thoughts and feelings today, we fact-check, we come back to our body and core, and we lean into positive thinking that affirms our safety and strength. Try other techniques alongside it and reach out for support if you need.

Tool seven – find your people

This tool can be applied in a lot of different ways. I'm not going to tell you precisely what to do, I'm just going to remind you that change and growth has a much better chance of becoming permanent if we find people who support these changes. Their support doesn't have to be explicit – they don't have to tell you, every day, that they support your growth. Their support can be implied by the way they give you space to do your own thing. They won't judge, they won't mock. Perhaps they model the changes you are trying to make, maybe because they've had their own journey, or perhaps because this is just who they are. Maybe they live the life you're aiming for, or maybe they're also on their own journey up and out of old patterns and reactions. Maybe you see a positivity and joy, self-belief, grit, resilience, sense of personal responsibility, commitment or emotional honesty in these people (your people) that inspires and motivates you.

Some people from your past will be able to travel with you, absolutely. Two of my closest friends are from school. Our friendships have been a journey. There have been difficult, painful moments, but ultimately these relationships demonstrate resilience, honesty and respect. We allow each other to grow and change. We allow each other to be imperfect. We have difficult conversations. We take space when we need it. We love deeply and loyally, but with gentleness too. They take responsibility for their own feelings and expect me to do the same. These two women have seen me at my lowest. They loved me through it (sometimes with dismay and exasperation, true). They've allowed me to transform into what I needed to become. This last point is critical – *your* people must allow you to become the brightest, fullest version of yourself. If their own egos or illness cannot allow them to do so, you must take the space you need. Do not remain stuck to make someone else feel better. Do not remain locked to dysfunction to please someone else. Do not let go of hope because of someone else's fear and despair.

One thing I hope this book has explained is that many people carry trauma. In fact, *most* people you know carry it in one form or another, but many of them – most of them – don't know it. I'm highlighting this because although my dearest hope for all humankind is that we collectively own our trauma, at the moment there is still a lot of misunderstanding. You and me, we're part of the future. We get it. We know its trauma and we call it that. But you're going to find that some people don't get it. And because of their own denial, fear and shame, they're going to take you down (even if they don't know they're doing it) as you grow and change.

Ask any ex-drinker. The friends and family who are the least supportive of their decision not to drink alcohol are dysfunctional drinkers. The people who react badly to someone else's decision not to drink are usually the ones reliant on alcohol themselves. So *of course* they're oh-so-triggered by people who move into sobriety. Unfortunately, you may experience similar triggered reactions as you break free from old trauma-led patterns and take responsibility for your healing. Your honesty and growth are going to trigger the people in your life who are stuck in old patterns and cycles. As you put down healthy boundaries in relationships, the people in your life who don't have healthy boundaries will be triggered. When you call it *trauma*, the people in your life who are deeply invested in minimising it and not calling it trauma are going to react. As you grow and change, some people (people entrenched in their own trauma or their dysfunction) are going to react (badly). Some will dismiss you. Some will laugh at you. Some will get angry. Some will avoid you. When this happens, please remember: It's not *about* you. Hand their reaction back to them. Don't hold it close. I know it feels personal, but it's not. Their reaction is about their life and their past. Most likely, they're triggered. *It is not about you – hand it back.*

If you find yourself without meaningful support, without role models, without flexible healthy relationships that can hold your growth, don't panic. This is what you do – detach from those in your life *with love* for now. Take some space from the old, unsupportive past relationships, and focus on forming new relationships that represent the future you want. Where are these *new* people?! They're everywhere; you just haven't found them yet. Some are taking part in hobbies that make their hearts sing. Loads are doing yoga, or going on retreats. Some are meditating or enrolling in a local mindfulness course. Others are taking a punt and setting up a new business. Many are reading self-help books or taking an online course in self-development. A lot are working with a therapist. Some are in one of the 12-step fellowships or in a local support group. Many of them (so many more than you think) are part of a local women's circle or men's circle. Others are signing up for self-development workshops. Loads of them are talking online with other people about how to grow and move forward. All of them are striving, learning and healing. They're taking responsibility for their feelings and reclaiming their lives.

These people are your people, so find them. You know where: in the healthy, new, joyful, empowered spaces and groups that you've always wanted to explore but have been too afraid to. Yes, the newness might feel uncomfortable. You might confuse healthy boundaries for rejection. Your low self-belief might be triggered by their healthy confidence. You might put them on a pedestal, and be shocked when they fall off it (which they will because they're fallible humans). You might feel hurt because they won't swoop in and 'fix' you. They will care for you, yes, but they will never take responsibility for your healing. Likewise, they won't ever expect you to take responsibility for their journey.

This will all feel hard at times, but it will empower you to grow.

The word I've said over and over and over again, as I try my best to explain what you're looking for in others, is *responsibility*. This is the word of this tool. You're looking for people who are taking responsibility for their healing, feelings, thoughts and actions. People who can own their feelings and not make them about you. People who can say sorry if they cross a line. People who can have a bad day (a terrible day) and neither hold you responsible for it nor expect you to fix it. People gently searching for health and growth, with no expectation that you will find it for them. This is respectful, empowering and adult. This (people taking personal responsibility) feels like paradise (once you get over the initial uncomfortable newness).

This willingness to take personal responsibility for their healing, feelings, thoughts and actions is what you're looking for in your people. *This* matters more than the fact they go on retreats or see a therapist. *This* is what will allow you to truly grow. So find *this* – and find your people.

Chapter Nine

Now what?

This book was meant to help you wake up. I wanted to puncture your consciousness, because this was how it worked for me. I had a lightbulb flash of a moment when I owned the fact that I had an eating disorder. Then later, another consciousness-puncturing moment when I understood that my dysfunctional coping and other symptoms were traumatic reactions. These truths are my own and they have guided this book. For those who needed a similar awakening, I hope this book has given you that. I hope you're awake and wanting more. Because I'm not saying *it's all trauma*, and then walking away, leaving you to hold that powerful truth. I'm saying *now that you know it's a reaction, you can heal*. No more pretending. No more denial. No more shame. Call it out, give it the death stare, so that you can reclaim your life.

This chapter has one main purpose: to inspire you to keep moving forward and commit to growth and healing. I hope this book serves to open the door to more consciousness, more clarity, more honesty in your life. There are certain truths that we can't 'untrue'. I couldn't *untrue* those consciousness-puncturing moments in my life that woke me up. I tried to ignore them but I couldn't, because these powerful realisations can't be undone. When an alcoholic has this moment of realisation, it ruins every drink they will ever have. The denial is punctured. They can't *untrue* the truth. My hope is that you're now in the same uncomfortable (hopeful, expansive, powerful) position having read this book.

Perhaps the truth that you can't *untrue* is that you carry trauma. Perhaps you lifted the lid on your childhood, and now see it for what it was. Perhaps your truth is that your relationships are being repeatedly damaged because of your triggered reactions. Perhaps your truth is that you have a major crutch that is damaging your mind and body. Perhaps you saw the damage your past has caused your working life and ability to succeed.

Whatever the truth is that you can't *untrue*, I hope you can transfer this to action.

The tools are a way to act on the truths you've uncovered, but my guess is that you'll need and want *more*. Have you had therapy? Some of you will have; some of you won't. I remember being so afraid of it. I had a deep subconscious fear that the therapist would uncover an evil, terrible, frightening truth about me. I feared they would tell me I was damaged beyond repair. I feared the connection and the depth that was required. I feared change. I feared support. I feared the idea of being truly seen. Some of you may think this sounds quite mad. But I suspect some of you really *get* what I'm saying.

This fear shows up in many colourful ways. We find excuses, we resist, we obfuscate, we judge the process and the therapist. We become perfectionists (*I'm waiting for the perfect therapist*). We become arrogant and egotistical (*of course I don't need therapy*). We put down those who have been brave enough to go to therapy and find many reasons that *they* are different to *us*. All this fear, all this colourful, dishonest resistance stops us from doing the one thing we really need to do . . .

. . . *go to therapy.*

The good, the bad and the ugly

In the first sentence of this book I told you that I've had some great, some good and some worryingly bad therapists over the years. I vividly remember a woefully inexperienced hypnotherapist, and how damaged and confused I felt as I left his practice room after a session that retraumatised me. Unfortunately, there have been others too.

If the professional trying to help you isn't engaged in their own therapeutic work, then they're unlikely to be able to help you in a meaningful way. They could even cause you harm. So we need to be able to find good therapists, who have looked honestly at their own past and their own dysfunction. People who haven't just done the obligatory counselling sessions they're required to do as part of their training to become a psychologist, counsellor or therapist, but who have undertaken real, deep, soul-searching work. If they haven't done this work, they're likely to bring all their baggage into the room.

I've sat in front of some of these people and something feels wrong. It feels confusing, disrespectful or just plain *off*. You get that icky feeling in your tummy – the one that warns you that your boundaries have been crossed somehow. You don't feel safe. You don't feel understood and connected. It feels like something isn't right. Your instinct picks up on the unspoken feelings that lie heavy in the room. But because of the power dynamic, many people just put up with it.

As well as finding a therapist, counsellor or psychologist who is engaged in their own therapeutic work, you also need to find someone who *understands trauma*. Please don't assume that they do understand it just because they're a professional. In an excellent democratic, grassroots turn-around, *you* now understand trauma. You understand how broad traumatic reactions can be and you know that trauma sits at the base of a lot of human dysfunction. You've learned how trauma can interfere with our relationships and you understand that trauma often leads to addiction and dysfunctional coping. You've seen how trauma can affect our ability to succeed and build fulfilling careers. You understand that trauma interferes with our mind and our body, and that both need to be healed. You know that trauma interferes with our self-beliefs and our understanding of the world. You *get* trauma, so finding a therapist who gets it will be much easier.

If you're unsure about a therapist's approach and experience, call them before the session. Ask what training they've had and how many years they've been working in trauma. Ask them to explain how and why trauma happens. If they won't, move on. If they can't, move on. If you don't like what you hear, move on.

Although I had some bad therapists, there were also some great ones. These great ones have changed my life, although they're such incredible therapists that they take absolutely no credit for the changes that have come about. They hand me back my gratitude and admiration, because they know that *I* changed things, not them. I did the work; they facilitated. I want to tell you their names, to put the spotlight on them; but I know that they don't need or want me to. The work they do helps heal the world, but they do it without fanfare. Their work has enabled me to write this book. It has enabled me to own my trauma, my life and myself. Working with a great therapist is a blessing, a joy and an honour. It's a collaboration. It's a journey and it's one that I dearly hope you go on when you're ready.

How to choose a psychologist, counsellor or therapist

Choosing a therapist – or type of therapy – can feel overwhelming. Because of this, I receive a lot of emails from people asking me to help them find a private therapist. Ten years ago, I would assist – I'd trawl through lists of psychologists and therapists in their town and send them a shortlist. Now, I say this:

Provided they've got the right credentials (i.e. they're a qualified psychotherapist, clinical psychologist or counsellor) and provided they treat trauma, the rest is about human connection. Literally, I want you to choose someone who feels good to you. You might warm to their photo or love the way they've done their website. Perhaps the way they've explained trauma really resonates with you. Or perhaps you feel really enthusiastic and interested as you read about them and their approach to treatment. When you talk to them on the phone it might feel scary, but you will feel a sense of trust and connection.

This might sound like an odd approach but it's actually very clever. Because these cues that your body is giving you (e.g. feeling good, warmth, positive internal reactions, enthusiasm, interest and openness, trust and connection) are signs that you feel safe.

You can see the 'best' trauma therapist in the world and if you don't feel safe it won't work. So, find someone you like and someone you can relate to. Don't choose the person you find intimidating and scary. Listen to your body – go where it feels safe. Although there may be times during the sessions where you're triggered and therefore feel unsafe, you should never feel unsafe because of the therapist. If you do, move on.

I know that many people don't have the option, financially, of seeing a private therapist, so what I've just written may be totally unrelatable. A lot of people also get in touch with me and ask how to navigate their public health systems. I can't give a precise guide here, as each system is different. But this, roughly, is what I say:

I believe most of us can find what we need within a good public health system, but it takes time and a willingness to keep pushing for what we need. If you don't like who you're initially referred to, go back to your GP and ask for another referral. Public healthcare systems require us to be proactive, which is extremely hard if we're feeling beaten down and low. But please try to find the strength to advocate for yourself. If this is too hard, ask a trusted friend or family member to advocate for you.

While you wait (often public health systems involve an infuriating, demoralising wait) help yourself however you can. Knowledge is power, so read every trauma book you can lay your hands on. Exercise. Do yoga. Eat well. Speak to trusted friends and family about your feelings and experience. Learn mindfulness and meditation if your symptoms will allow. Use the tools in this book, and other self-help tools, to manage your symptoms. Go to local support groups or one of the 12-step fellowships if your coping is making things worse. Don't give up. Keep moving forward, until the right clinical support is available to you.

Try it all on

Trauma healing happens in a gentle spiral. We start with what feels comfortable and we work towards the centre of the hurt, in our own time. The nearer the centre we get, the deeper we go into our trauma, our subconscious and our pain. Deep therapeutic work is different for everyone, but it always involves a challenging, honest, exploration of ourselves. We do it when our minds and bodies are ready. Deep work brings about deep healing. Our body and our mind open up to us, and we slowly uncover truths that bring with them fundamental shifts. Deep work challenges us to help us grow. It challenges us to empower us. It should be confronting – that's kind of the point – but it should also be safe, accepting and kind.

Here, I really need to highlight that you can't *only* do deep therapeutic work. It would be unnecessary and too much . . . plus you'd become a self-obsessed hermit. Periods of challenging, deep work must be balanced with periods of lightness and gentleness. Growth can, and should, be fun. There's challenging newness, but within that newness is the stuff that will make your heart sing. It's about finding glorious new relationships, it's starting hobbies that make you feel true joy, it's getting a new job or starting a business that really *feels* good. It's looking after and appreciating your body. It's learning about your own sexuality and needs. It's leaning into healthy femininity and masculinity. It's exploration and adventure. It's allowing yourself to try everything on and see what feels good as you rebuild your connection to yourself and the world.

As I write, I'm looking at some of the books I bought when I was exploring shamanism about eight years ago. Shamanism – an ancient spiritual practice designed to alter states of consciousness and connect with ancestral spirits – wasn't for me, but oh, I loved learning about it. I love that I was brave enough to go and sit with shamans. I listened to them and learnt from them. Ultimately, this wasn't for me, but dipping my toes into this alternative aspect of healing was awesome (this really is the right word). I'm absolutely not saying that you *should* find a shaman. My interest in shamanism was driven by my unending thirst for knowledge about how humans heal. I'm not suggesting it as a possible treatment for trauma – it's not. What I'm saying is that you're allowed to explore. It's *your* journey of recovery and discovery. I couldn't possibly list all the alternative treatments out there that wonderful, creative humans have put their heart and soul into developing. From different types of massage to reiki, from essential oils to meditation, from chakra work to naturopathy, from crystals to sage. If it feels safe and nourishing, consider it. If it feels unsafe and damaging, walk away. Explore different healing modalities because in the exploration comes great knowledge and (all together now!) fun.

Now what?!

It's up to you. You know what you need. Go back to those intentions you set in tool one. What are you seeking? What do you want? What do you need? You decide on your next step, because it's your journey.

With love,

S. x

Where to find me

Before I sign off, I want to remind you that I'm a real person who genuinely wants to help. If you want to work with me, or just want to get in touch, you can contact me through my website or on social media:

www.sarahwoodhouse.com
@thesarahwoodhouse on Facebook and Instagram
@sn_woodhouse on Twitter

S. x

Appendix

Common trauma symptoms

Below are some of the common, uniform traumatic symptoms that are well known and consistently appear as responses to a traumatic experience. They *are* your trauma. They *are* your survival response to a perceived threat. They're a mix of physiological, emotional, cognitive and behavioural reactions. Many are instant (i.e. they occur as the survival response kicks in); others, like being easily stressed out, emerge over time. You may have experienced a few of these, or you may have experienced many.

- Physical sensations such as a racing heart, sweating, tingling, nausea
- Dissociation (i.e. feeling spacey, floaty and out of body)
- Being easily startled and jumpy

- Feeling *on guard* all the time
- Difficulty sleeping
- Difficulty concentrating
- Racing mind and repetitive thoughts
- Nightmares and night terrors
- Shame or lack of self-worth
- Feeling emotionally numb and shutdown
- Easily stressed out
- Intrusive memories, images, thoughts or 'flashbacks' related to the past experience
- Consistently negative thoughts and/or feelings about yourself, others and the world
- Abrupt mood swings or consistently low mood
- Avoiding people, places, activities, memories, thoughts or feelings that remind you of the experience.

A few of these symptoms experienced often, to the extreme and in response to the same triggers, indicates there may be a past trauma. If you experience multiple symptoms you may have a high level of trauma symptoms (i.e. PTSD). If you believe you have high symptom levels, please book an appointment with a trauma-informed therapist or speak to your GP. This book is not intended as a substitute for therapeutic, medical or clinical care. I encourage you to get the help you need if you need it.

Resources

Resources

If you are experiencing high levels of trauma symptoms and/or PTSD please contact your local doctor for a treatment referral or use one of the urgent support phonelines below if you need help now.

Visit one of the following organisations website for more information about PTSD.

Australia:

Blue Knot Foundation

blueknot.org.au

Phoenix Australia

phoenixaustralia.org

Black Dog Institute
blackdoginstitute.org.au/resources-support/
post-traumatic-stress-order/

For urgent support, call Lifeline on 13 11 14 for
confidential 24/7 counselling and referrals.

UK:
Mind
mind.org.uk/information-support/types-of-mental-
health-problems/post-traumatic-stress-disorder-ptsd/
about-ptsd/

The Royal College of Psychiatrists
rcpsych.ac.uk/mental-health/problems-
disorders/post-traumatic-stress-disorder

NHS
nhs.uk/conditions/post-traumatic-stress-
disorder-ptsd/

For urgent support, call Samaritans on 116 123 for
confidential 24/7 support.

USA:
National Centre for PTSD
ptsd.va.gov/index.asp

Mayo Clinic

mayoclinic.org/diseases-conditions/post-traumatic-stress-disorder/symptoms-causes/syc-20355967

For urgent support, please contact National Suicide Prevention Lifeline on 1800 273 TALK.

Trauma jargon (Glossary)

Adrenaline

A hormone produced by the adrenal glands in response to a stressor or threat, as well as at other times (see *cortisol* and *noradrenaline* for other fight or flight hormones). Among other things, adrenaline increases our heart rate, blood flow to our muscles and enlarges the pupils in our eyes to prepare the body for fight or flight (e.g. vigorous action). Also called 'epinephrine'.

Amygdala

Two small, almond-shaped parts of the brain (one in each hemisphere) that play an important role in emotion and behaviour. The amygdala has many functions, but is best known for its role in processing fear. When it senses a threat, the amygdala triggers our fight or flight survival response – first in the hypothalamus and then throughout the *HPA axis* (see below).

Autonomic nervous system

The autonomic nervous system (ANS) is one of our body's control systems, and largely acts unconsciously (i.e. we're not consciously aware of what it's up to at any given moment). There are two main branches of the nervous system: the sympathetic nervous system (SNS) and the parasympathetic nervous system (PNS). The SNS is the quick response arousal system that's activated during the fight or flight response. The PNS, most often, plays the opposite role – it activates more slowly and dampens/slows down bodily functions and responses.

Body work

Techniques that help our body, nervous system and energy to rebalance. Examples of body work are reiki, yoga, breathwork, touch work, tai chi, Bowen therapy and kinesiology. Some types of body work also incorporate aspects of psychotherapy. This is referred to in the book as *somatic psychotherapy* (see pp. 232 to 233).

Cognitive

High-level mental processes that relate to cognition (e.g. thinking, knowing, problem-solving).

Cognitive Behavioural Therapy (CBT)

A short-term, goal-oriented type of psychotherapy which aims to change unhelpful patterns of thinking and behaviour. CBT is used by many public healthcare systems to treat a wide range of issues (e.g. anxiety, depression, relationship problems, addiction). It focuses on changing the underlying thoughts and beliefs (cognitive processes) that drive unhelpful attitudes and behaviours.

Cortisol

A hormone produced by the adrenal glands in response to a stressor or threat, as well as at other times (see *adrenaline* and *noradrenaline* for other fight or flight hormones). It's often referred to as the 'stress hormone' because it's a central part of the body's fight or flight response. It serves many functions, including controlling our blood sugar levels and regulating our metabolism. But as part of the fight or flight response it curbs bodily functions that are nonessential (e.g. alters the immune system responses and suppresses the digestive system). If triggered regularly, high levels of cortisol can cause long-term damage to our body (see pp. 137 to 138).

Eye Movement Desensitization and Reprocessing (EMDR)

A type of psychotherapy that helps people heal from the symptoms and emotional distress that result from disturbing life experiences. The treatment uses a person's own rapid eye movements to dampen the power of traumatic memories. It's widely used to treat PTSD and was designed by Dr Francine Shapiro.

HPA (Hypothalamic–pituitary–adrenal) axis
A complex set of interactions between the hypothalamus (in the brain) and the pituitary and adrenal glands (in the body). Along with our autonomic nervous system, the HPA axis controls our reaction to stress. It also regulates many bodily processes (e.g. the immune system and our emotions).

Neuroplasticity
Refers to the brain's ability to reorganise itself by forming new neural pathways throughout life. It has significant implications for learning, healing and development and recovery from brain damage.

Noradrenaline
A hormone produced by the adrenal glands in response to a stressor or threat, as well as at other times (see *cortisol* and *adrenaline* for other fight or flight hormones). It mobilises the brain and body for action – increasing alertness and arousal and promoting vigilance. Also called 'norepinephrine'.

Polyvagal breathing
A type of rhythmic diaphragmatic breathing that stimulates the vagus nerve, therefore helping our nervous system and body rebalance after a stress response. The breathing stems from Dr Stephen Porges' *polyvagal theory* (see below). In

this book, I describe two types of polyvagal breathing: '4/8' and 'voo'.

4/8 involves inhaling deep into the belly for the count of four, then exhaling for the count of eight. I have specified a 4/8 count, but other counts will serve the same purpose. Some somatic practitioners recommend a 4/10 count, others recommend a 3/6 count. There are many variations – find one that works for you. What matters is that there's a rhythm, and that the breath moves down through the diaphragm into the belly.

Voo involves inhaling deep into the belly, and on the exhale making a deep, long 'voooooooooooo' noise from the depths of your belly. The vibration is very soothing and stimulates the vagus nerve.

Polyvagal theory
Introduced by Dr Stephen Porges, this theory focuses on the role of the vagus nerve in the fear response, as well as emotion regulation and social connection. It's been influential within many types of somatic psychotherapy.

Somatic
Relating to, or affecting, the body.

Somatic psychotherapy
A type of psychotherapy that includes body-focused techniques, alongside more traditional talking methods. This is done to help the body release trapped trauma. These types of therapy are focused on increasing the mind–body

connection, and most practitioners believe that the mind and body must be viewed as one. Somatic psychotherapists believe that the body wants to heal, and can heal, if given the right environment and support. Also called 'body psychotherapy' or 'body-oriented psychotherapy'.

Trauma Loop

A cycle of physical, emotional, cognitive and behavioural reactions fuelled by the survival (fight, flight, freeze) response to threat. These reactions feed into each other, often heightening each other's intensity. This loop of reactions prevents us from connecting with our body, the essential part of our being and our adult self.

Traumatic beliefs

The subconscious conclusions we come to about ourselves and the world during our ongoing traumatic reaction. They're one of the cognitive outcomes of our sense of threat, the fight or flight response, our overwhelm and sense of powerlessness. These beliefs are easily triggered, but unlike other more obvious reactions (e.g. anxiety) we're often unaware that these damaging beliefs are operating.

Traumatic coping

This refers to any dysfunctional behavioural strategies we use to cope with our traumatic reaction. Drinking alcohol, compulsive distraction (e.g. watching TV or checking your phone), compulsive busyness (e.g. tidying, making plans), over-eating and binging, under-eating, people-pleasing, compulsive spending, risky sexual behaviour, avoiding intimacy and touch, self-harm, drug use and watching porn can all be considered traumatic coping. These types of coping locks us into the Trauma Loop, whereas healthy coping helps us break free.

Traumatic reactions

Most psychologists use this term only to refer to core trauma symptoms (see Appendix). In this book, and in all the work I do, I use this term to refer to the broader physical, emotional, cognitive or behavioural reactions to our trauma. I do this to help us be compassionate with ourselves and others. So much dysfunction is caused by trauma, so of course it's appropriate to acknowledge that these painful outcomes are often reactions to something from our past. For example, using alcohol to cope with trauma shows us that, in this context, alcoholism is part of the traumatic reaction, not separate to it.

Traumatic thinking

The patterns of thinking we develop as a result of the sense of threat, the overwhelm and the flood of fight or flight hormones into our mind. Repetitive negative thinking, extreme negative thoughts about ourselves and the world, black and white thinking, rumination and worry are all examples of traumatic thinking. Over time, this kind of thinking becomes habitual and further traps us into the Trauma Loop.

Trigger

A trigger is something that reminds us of a past trauma, and which triggers (sets off) our traumatic reaction. Triggers can be anything: a smell, a person, a word, an image, a sound, a situation, a tone of voice . . . anything that our mind has associated with a past trauma.

Vagus nerve

The longest nerve in the whole autonomic nervous system, running from the brain, through the face and thorax, down into the abdomen. It's part of the parasympathetic branch of the nervous system and carries out various functions from heart rate to muscle movements in the mouth (including speech). In recent years, thanks to polyvagal theory, the nerve has been recognised as playing an important role in the survival response. If the sympathetic branch of the autonomic nervous system is highly aroused (as it is during stress and trauma), the vagus nerve can become overstimulated and 'put the brakes on' the nervous system. This can lead to the symptoms associated with the 'freeze' response (e.g. shutdown, dissociation).

Importantly, the nerve is also now recognised for its ability to help us regulate our stress and triggered reactions (see *polyvagal breathing*, pp. 231 to 232).

Notes

Introduction

1. Here's a selection of studies and reviews that demonstrate the association between different types of trauma and various mental health and wellbeing outcomes:

Aas, M., Henry, C., Andreassen, O., Bellivier, F., Melle, I., Etain, B. (2016). The role of childhood trauma in bipolar disorders, *International Journal of Bipolar Disorders*, Vol. 4.

Hovens J. G. F. M., et al. (2010). Childhood life events and childhood trauma in adult patients with depressive, anxiety and comorbid disorders vs controls, *Acta Psychiatrica Scandinavica*, Vol. 22(1).

Kendler, K. S., Bulik, C. M., Silberg, J. (2000). Childhood sexual abuse and adult psychiatric and substance use disorders in women: An epidemiological and cotwin control analysis, *Archives of General Psychiatry*, Vol. 57(10).

Kendler, K. S., et al. (1993). The prediction of major depression in women: Towards an integrated etiological model. *American Journal of Psychiatry*, Vol. 150.

Kuo, J. R., Goldin, P. R., Werner, K., Heimberg, R. G., Gross, J. J. (2011). Childhood trauma and current psychological functioning in adults with social anxiety disorder, *Journal of Anxiety Disorders*, Vol. 25(4).

McCauley, J., Kern, D. E., Kolodner, K. (1997). Clinical characteristics of women with a history of child abuse, *JAMA*, Vol. 277(17).

Royse, D., Rompf, B. L., Dhooper, S. S. (1991). Childhood trauma and adult life satisfaction in a random adult sample, *Psychological Reports*, Vol. 69(3 Pt 2).

Stein, M. B., et al. (1996). Childhood physical and sexual abuse in patients with anxiety disorders in a community sample, *American Journal of Psychiatry*, Vol. 153(2).

Whisman, M. A. (2006). Childhood trauma and marital outcomes in adulthood. *Personal Relationships*, Vol. 13(4).

2 Felitti, V. J., et al. (1998). Relationship of childhood abuse and household dysfunction to many of the leading causes of death in adults: the Adverse Childhood Experiences (ACE) study, *American Journal of Preventative Medicine*, Vol. 14. The study included ten categories of Adverse Childhood Experiences. Please see pages 135 to 136 in chapter five for all ten categories.

3 Burke Harris, N. (2018). *Toxic Childhood Stress: The legacy of early trauma and how to heal*, Bluebird, London.

Felitti et al., Relationship of childhood abuse and household dysfunction to many of the leading causes of death in adults: The Adverse Childhood Experiences (ACE) study.

4 Copeland, W. E., Shanahan, L. Hinesley, J. (2018). Association of childhood trauma exposure with adult psychiatric disorders and functional outcomes, *JAMA*, Vol. 1(7).

Felitti et al., Relationship of childhood abuse and household dysfunction to many of the leading causes of death in adults: the Adverse Childhood Experiences (ACE) study.

Goodwin, R. et al. (2003). Association between childhood physical abuse and gastrointestinal disorders and migraine in adulthood, *American Journal of Public Health,* Vol. 93(7).

For an overview, see Van der kolk, B. (2003) The neurobiology of childhood trauma and abuse, *Child and Adolescent Psychiatric Clinics*, Vol. 12(2).

See also note 1 above for other studies in this area.

Chapter One

1 The Hoffman Institute, 'Trauma, resilience and addiction: Hoffman interviews Dr Gabor Maté', 19 January 2021, hoffmaninstitute.co.uk/trauma-resilience-and-addiction-hoffman-interviews-dr-gabor-mate/.

2 Levine, P. (2018). *Healing Trauma: A pioneering program for restoring the wisdom of your body*, Sounds True, Boulder, CO.

3 Dr Francine Shapiro was the creator of Eye Movement Desensitization and Reprocessing (EMDR – see glossary). For an accessible overview of Dr Shapiro's techniques, see Shapiro, F. (2013). *Getting Past Your Past: Take control of your life with self-help techniques from EMDR therapy*, Rodale, New York.

4 Reflects the work of Anke Ehlers and David Clark in Ehlers, A., Clark, D. (2000). A cognitive model of posttraumatic stress disorder, *Behavioural Research and Therapy*, Vol. 15(3). This paper was highly influential in the rise of Cognitive Behavioural Therapy (CBT – see glossary) as a treatment for trauma.

5 Janoff-Bulman, R. (1992). *Shattered Assumptions: Towards a new psychology of trauma*, Simon & Schuster, New York.

6 Maté, G. (2018). *In the Realm of Hungry Ghosts: Close encounters with addiction*, Random House, UK.

7 See Levine, P., Kline, M. (2008). *Trauma-Proofing Your Kids: A Parents Guide for Instilling Confidence, Joy and Resilience*, North Atlantic Books, New York. If you are concerned that your child has experienced a trauma, please contact your local doctor or a trauma-informed child psychologist or psychotherapist.

8 American Psychiatric Association. (2013). *Diagnostic and Statistical Manual of Mental Disorders*, 5th edition, APA, Arlington, VA.

9 Weathers, F. W., Blake, D. D., Schnurr, P. P., Kaloupek, D. G., Marx, B. P., Keane, T. M. (2013). *The Life Events Checklist for DSM-5 (LEC-5)*. Instrument available from the National Center for PTSD at ptsd.va.gov. Levine, P. (2018). *Healing Trauma: A pioneering program for restoring the wisdom of your body*.
In line with current research and theory, I've included birth and bereavement on the big-T trauma list.

10 Kilpatrick, D. G. (2013). National estimates of exposure to traumatic events and PTSD prevalence using DSM-IV and DSM-5 criteria, *Journal of Traumatic Stress*, Vol. 26(5).

11 Levine, P. (1997). *Waking the Tiger: Healing trauma: the innate capacity to transform overwhelming experiences*, North Atlantic Books, Berkeley.

12 Levine, P. (2018). *Healing Trauma: A pioneering program for restoring the wisdom of your body*, p. 8.

13 Tang, W., Hu, T., Hu, B., Jin, C., Wang, G., Xie, C., Chen, S., Xu, J. (2020). Prevalence and correlates of PTSD and depressive symptoms

one month after the outbreak of the COVID-19 epidemic in a sample of home-quarantined Chinese university students. *Journal of Affective Disorders*, Vol 274, pp. 1–7.

14 Please be aware that the polyvagal 4/8 count is a guide rather than a strict rule. All that matters is that the exhale is longer than the inhale, and that you're breathing deeply into your belly/diaphragm. I often use a 4/10 count; some prefer a 3/6 count. Find what works best for you.

15 Porges, S. (2017). *The Pocket Guide to The Polyvagal Theory: The transformative power of feeling safe*, W.W. Norton & Company, New York.

Levine, P. (2010). *In an Unspoken Voice: How the body releases trauma and restores goodness*, North Atlantic Books, Berkeley.

16 Breslau, N., Chilcoat, H. D., Kessler, R. C., Davis, G. C. (1999). Previous exposure to trauma and PTSD effects of subsequent trauma: Results from the Detroit Area Survey of Trauma, *American Journal of Psychiatry*, Vol. 156(6).

Chapter Two

1 Brown, B, 'Listening to Shame', TED, 3 December 2020, ted.com/talks/brene_brown_listening_to_shame/up-next?language=en.

Brown, B. (2020). *The Gifts of Imperfection: Let go of who you think you're supposed to be and embrace who you are*, 10th anniversary edition, Vermillion, London.

2 Bauer, P. J., Larkina, M. (2014). The onset of childhood amnesia: a prospective investigation of the course and determinants of forgetting of early-life events, *Public Access*, Vol, 22(8).

3 Yehuda, R., Halligan, S. L., Bierer, L. M. (2001). Relationship of parental trauma exposure and PTSD to PTSD, depressive and anxiety disorders in offspring, *Journal of Psychiatric Research*, Vol. 35(5).

4 Iyengar, U. (2014). Unresolved trauma in mothers: intergenerational effects and the role of reorganization. *Frontiers in Psychology*, Vol. 5.

5   National Human Genome Research Institute, 'Epigenetics', 3 December 2020, genome.gov/genetics-glossary/Epigenetics.

6 Dias, B. G., Ressler, K. J. (2014). Parental olfactory experience influences behaviour and neural structure in subsequent generations, *Nature Neuroscience*, Vol. 17(1).

Chapter Three

1 Porges, S. (2017). *The Pocket Guide to the Polyvagal Theory: The transformative power of feeling safe*, W. W. Norton & Company, New York.

2   Katie, B. (2002). *Loving What Is: Four questions that can change your life*, Rider, London.

3   Walker, P. 'The 4Fs: A trauma typology in complex PTSD', 3 December 2020, pete-walker.com/fourFs_TraumaTypologyComplexPTSD.htm.

4   World Health Organization. (2018). *International classification of diseases for mortality and morbidity statistics*, 11th revision. The C-PTSD diagnosis was added to the ICD-10 in 2018.

5   For an overview, see UK National Health Service, 'Complex PTSD', 3 December 2020, nhs.uk/conditions/post-traumatic-stress-disorder-ptsd/complex/.

Chapter Four

1   Breslau, N., Chilcoat, H. D., Kessler, R. C., Davis, G. C. (1999). Previous exposure to trauma and PTSD effects of subsequent trauma: Results from the Detroit Area Survey of Trauma, *American Journal of Psychiatry*, Vol. 156(6).

Chapter Five

1   Arousal and satiation highs are described in Nakken, C. (1996). *The Addictive Personality: Understanding the addictive process and compulsive behaviour*, 2nd edition, Hazelden, Centre City, Minn, p. 3. Deprivation high is described in Carnes, P. (2019). *The Betrayal Bond: Breaking free of exploitative relationships*, rev edition, Health Communications Inc, Deerfield Beach.

2   Nakken, *The Addictive Personality: Understanding the addictive process and compulsive behaviour*.

3   Nakken, *The Addictive Personality: Understanding the addictive process and compulsive behaviour*, p. 5.

4   For a selection of up-to-date research into neuroplasticity, see Science Direct, 'Neural Plasticity', 3 December 2020, sciencedirect.com/topics/medicine-and-dentistry/neural-plasticity.

5   Burke Harris, N. (2018). *Toxic Childhood Stress: The legacy of early trauma and how to heal*, Bluebird, London.

6   Levine, P. (2010). *In an Unspoken Voice: How the body releases trauma and restores goodness*, North Atlantic Books, Berkeley.

7   Felitti, J., et al. (1998). Relationship of childhood abuse and household dysfunction to many of the leading causes of death in adults:

the Adverse Childhood Experiences (ACE) study, *American Journal of Preventative Medicine,* Vol. 14.

8   Burke Harris, *Toxic Childhood Stress,* p. 39.

9   For an overview, see Institute for Chronic Pain, 'Trauma', 3 December 2020, instituteforchronicpain.org/understanding-chronic-pain/complications/trauma.

10 Shapiro, F. (2013). *Getting Past Your Past: Take control of your life with self-help techniques from EMDR,* Rodale, New York.

Chapter Seven

1   Tedeshi, R. G., Calhoun, L. G. (1996). The Posttraumatic Growth Inventory: Measuring the positive legacy of trauma, *Journal of Traumatic Stress,* Vol. 9(3).

2   Oxford University Press, Lexico, 3 December 2020, lexico.com/definition/spirituality.

3   American Psychological Association, 'Building your resilience', 3 December 2020, apa.org/helpcenter/road-resilience.

4   Dweck, C. (2017). *Mindset: Changing the way you think to fulfil your potential,* rev edition, Robinson, London.

Chapter Eight

1   Levine, P. (1997). *Waking the Tiger: Healing trauma: the innate capacity to transform overwhelming experiences,* North Atlantic Books, Berkeley.

Bibliography

Aas, M., Henry, C., Andreassen, O., Bellivier, F., Melle, I., Etain, B. (2016). The role of childhood trauma in bipolar disorders, *International Journal of Bipolar Disorders*, Vol. 4.

American Psychiatric Association. (2013). *Diagnostic and Statistical Manual of Mental Disorders*, 5th edition, APA, Arlington, VA.

American Psychological Association, 'Building your resilience', 3 December 2020, apa.org/helpcenter/road-resilience.

Bauer, P. J., Larkina, M. (2014). The onset of childhood amnesia: a prospective investigation of the course and determinants of forgetting of early-life events, *Public Access*, Vol. 22(8).

Breslau, N., Chilcoat, H. D., Kessler, R. C., Davis, G. C. (1999). Previous exposure to trauma and PTSD effects of subsequent trauma: Results from the Detroit Area Survey of Trauma, *American Journal of Psychiatry*, Vol. 156(6).

Brown, B., 'Listening to Shame', TED, 3 December 2020, ted.com/talks/brene_brown_listening_to_shame/up-next?language=en.

Brown, B. (2020). *The Gifts of Imperfection: Let go of who you think you're supposed to be and embrace who you are*, 10th anniversary edition, Vermillion, London.

Bibliography

Burke Harris, N. (2018). *Toxic Childhood Stress: The legacy of early trauma and how to heal*, Bluebird, London.

Carnes, P. (2019). *The Betrayal Bond: Breaking free of exploitative relationships*, rev edition, Health Communications Inc, Deerfield Beach.

Copeland, W. E., Shanahan, L. Hinesley, J. (2018). Association of childhood trauma exposure with adult psychiatric disorders and functional outcomes, *JAMA*, Vol. 1(7).

Dias, B. G., Ressler, K. J. (2014). Parental olfactory experience influences behaviour and neural structure in subsequent generations, *Nature Neuroscience*, Vol. 17(1).

Dweck, C. (2017). *Mindset: Changing the way you think to fulfil your potential*, rev edition, Robinson, London.

Ehlers, A., Clark, D. (2000). A cognitive model of posttraumatic stress disorder, *Behavioural Research and Therapy*, Vol. 15(3).

Elliot, D. M., Briere, J. (1992). Sexual abuse trauma among professional women: validating the Trauma Symptom Checklist-40 (TSC-40), *Child Abuse & Neglect*, Vol. 16(3).

Felitti, V. J., et al. (1998). Relationship of childhood abuse and household dysfunction to many of the leading causes of death in adults: the Adverse Childhood Experiences (ACE) study, *American Journal of Preventative Medicine*, Vol. 14.

Goodwin, R. et al. (2003). Association between childhood physical abuse and gastrointestinal disorders and migraine in adulthood, *American Journal of Public Health*, Vol. 93(7).

Hovens J. G. F. M., et al. (2010). Childhood life events and childhood trauma in adult patients with depressive, anxiety and comorbid disorders vs controls, *Acta Psychiatrica Scandinavica*, Vol. 22(1).

Institute for Chronic Pain, 'Trauma', 3 December 2020, instituteforchronicpain.org/understanding-chronic-pain/complications/trauma.

Iyengar, U. (2014). Unresolved trauma in mothers: intergenerational effects and the role of reorganization. *Frontiers in Psychology*, Vol. 5.

Janoff-Bulman, R. (1992). *Shattered Assumptions: Towards a new psychology of trauma*, Simon & Schuster, New York.

Katie, B. (2002). *Loving What Is: Four questions that can change your life*, Rider, London.

Kendler, K. S., Bulik, C. M., Silberg, J. (2000). Childhood sexual abuse and adult psychiatric and substance use disorders in women: An epidemiologicalandcotwincontrolanalysis,*ArchivesofGeneralPsychiatry*, Vol. 57(10).

Kendler, K. S., et al. (1993). The prediction of major depression in women: Towards an integrated etiological model, *American Journal of Psychiatry*, Vol. 150.

Kilpatrick, D. G. (2013). National estimates of exposure to traumatic events and PTSD prevalence using DSM-IV and DSM-5 criteria, *Journal of Traumatic Stress*, Vol. 26(5).

Kuo, J. R., Goldin, P. R., Werner, K., Heimberg, R. G., Gross, J. J. (2011). Childhood trauma and current psychological functioning in adult with social anxiety disorder, *Journal of Anxiety Disorders*, Vol. 25(4).

Levine, P. (2018). *Healing Trauma: A pioneering program for restoring the wisdom of your body*, Sounds True, Boulder, CO.

Levine, P. (2010). *In an Unspoken Voice: How the body releases trauma and restores goodness*, North Atlantic Books, Berkeley.

Levine, P. (1997). *Waking the Tiger: Healing trauma: the innate capacity to transform overwhelming experiences*, North Atlantic Books, Berkeley.

Levine, P., Kline, M. (2008). *Trauma Proofing Your Kids: A parents' guide for instilling confidence, joy and resilience* North Atlantic Books, New York.

Maté, G. (2018). *In the Realm of Hungry Ghosts: Close encounters with addiction* Random House, UK.

McCauley, J., Kern, D. E., Kolodner, K. (1997). Clinical characteristic of women with a history of child abuse, *JAMA*, Vol. 277(17).

Nakken, C. (1996). *The Addictive Personality: Understanding the addictive process and compulsive behaviour*, 2nd edition, Hazelden, Centre City, Minn.

National Human Genome Research Institute, 'Epigenetics', 3 December 2020, genome.gov/genetics-glossary/Epigenetics.

Oxford University Press, Lexico, 3 December 2020, lexico.com/definition/spirituality.

Porges, S. (2017). *The Pocket Guide to The Polyvagal Theory: The transformative power of feeling safe*, W.W. Norton & Company, New York.

Royse, D., Rompf, B. L., Dhooper, S. S. (1991). Childhood trauma and adult life satisfaction in a random adult sample, *Psychological Reports*, Vol. 69(3 Pt 2).

Science Direct, 'Neural Plasticity', 3 December 2020, sciencedirect.com/topics/medicine-and-dentistry/neural-plasticity.

Bibliography

Shapiro, F. (2013). *Getting Past Your Past: Take control of your life with self-help techniques from EMDR therapy*, Rodale, New York.

Stein, M. B., et al. (1996). Childhood physical and sexual abuse in patients with anxiety disorders in a community sample, *American Journal of Psychiatry*, Vol. 153(2).

Tang, W., Hu, T., Hu, B., Jin, C., Wang, G., Xie, C., Chen, S., Xu, J. (2020). Prevalence and correlates of PTSD and depressive symptoms one month after the outbreak of the COVID-19 epidemic in a sample of home-quarantined Chinese university students. *Journal of Affective Disorders*, Vol. 274, pp. 1–7.

Tedeshi, R. G., Calhoun, L. G. (1996). The Posttraumatic Growth Inventory: measuring the positive legacy of trauma, *Journal of Traumatic Stress*, Vol. 9(3).

UK National Health Service, 'Complex PTSD', 3 December 2020, nhs.uk/conditions/post-traumatic-stress-disorder-ptsd/complex/.

Van der kolk, B. (2003). The neurobiology of childhood trauma and abuse, *Child and Adolescent Psychiatric Clinics*, Vol. 12(2).

Walker, P. 'The 4Fs: A trauma typology in complex PTSD', 3 December 2020, pete-walker.com/fourFs_TraumaTypologyComplexPTSD.htm.

Weathers, F. W., Blake, D. D., Schnurr, P. P., Kaloupek, D. G., Marx, B. P., Keane, T. M. (2013). *The Life Events Checklist for DSM-5 (LEC-5)*. Instrument available from the National Center for PTSD at ptsd.va.gov.

Whisman, M. A. (2006). Childhood trauma and marital outcomes in adulthood. *Personal Relationships*, Vol. 13(4).

World Health Organization (2018). *International classification of diseases for mortality and morbidity statistics*, 11th revision. The C-PTSD diagnosis was added to the ICD-10 in 2018.

Yehuda, R., Halligan, S. L., Bierer. (2001). Relationship of parental trauma exposure and PTSD to PTSD, depressive and anxiety disorders in offspring, *Journal of Psychiatric Research*, Vol. 35(5).

Acknowledgements

I want to thank the many people who, in one way or another, helped create this book. First, I want to thank my husband, Neil, who has supported my work and my ideas from the moment we met. Your passion for the messages in this book gave me the confidence to keep writing. *Thank you doesn't quite seem enough, but it's all I've got – so, thank you.*

A huge heartfelt thank you to Sophie Ambrose, at Penguin Random House, for your endless support, and for your sense of humour. Thank you also to Kalhari Jayaweera at Penguin Random House for your thoughtful contributions to the book. And to the whole PRH team – thank you.

I want to thank Lisa Moylett and Zoë Apostolides, at CMM literary agency. Your support, enthusiasm and tenacity helped make this book a reality – thank you.

Thank you also to my first editor, Anjanette Fennell. Your worldly wisdom about the publishing industry ensured this book became a book! Thank you.

A huge thank you to Shardai di Giorgio, who looked after my children with such love as I wrote (and wrote and wrote). What an incredible woman you are, thank you. And thank you to Dian Henson-Shields, who also helped look after my noisy brood, and who inspired me to write an accessible book on trauma.

Thank you to my wonderful mum and dad, who helped me believe I could do anything I put my mind to – this book is proof of that belief.

I want to thank Deborah Maloney-Marsden (one of the *great* therapists), the 12-step fellowships and all who have supported me in recovery. I'm standing on your shoulders. Thank you.

A huge sisterly thank you to Sally Cumberland for showing up for me when it matters most. You bring so much grace, recovery, laughter, wisdom and love into my life – thank you. And to Nova Maxwell, Laura Bailey and Debbie Brogan: your support and love mean everything to me, thank you.

Thank you all, from the bottom of my heart. x

Index

Index

Index

Index

Index

Discover a
new favourite

Visit **penguin.com.au/readmore**